MANORS & MAYHEM, PAUPERS & PARSONS

TALES FROM FOUR SHIRES:
Buckinghamshire, Bedfordshire, Hertfordshire & Northamptonshire

by
John Houghton

All Royalties to
WILLEN
HOSPICE

First published October 1996
by
The Book Castle
12 Church Street
Dunstable
Bedfordshire LU5 4RU

ISBN 1 871199 18 2

Front Cover: The murder of the Archbishop of Canterbury,
Thomas à Beckett, in 1170.

Computer typeset by Keyword, Aldbury, Hertfordshire.
Printed by Progressive Printing (UK) Ltd., Leigh-on-Sea, Essex.

CONTENTS

The de Medici Room, Gayhurst, where the Gunpoweder Plot was hatched.
(JH)

PREFACE

Here are more true tales from the fascinating history of mid-Anglia – astonishing, shocking, intriguing and sometimes heart-warming.

'Manors and Mayhem, Paupers and Parsons' tells of the part played in local and national history by great houses – but it also tells of ordinary folk, and the often extraordinary things they do – or have done to them! Much has changed over the 1,000 years covered in this book, but there is one continuing factor which does not change – human nature!

As Robert Burns once wrote:

'The social friendly, honest man
Whate'er he be
'Tis he fulfils great Nature's plan
And none but he!'

ABOUT THE AUTHOR

John Houghton was born in Eastbourne in 1916. After graduating at Durham University he was ordained in 1939 and was Curate at Wolverton (1939–42). From 1942 to 1973 he served in Northern Rhodesia/Zambia and was awarded the Zambian Order of Distinguished Service in 1966. He is a Canon Emeritus of Lusaka Cathedral. He retired in 1983 and lives in Bletchley.

Also by John Houghton:
Borrowed Time Extended
Tales from Milton Keynes
Murders & Mysteries, People & Plots
Eccentrics & Villains, Hauntings & Heroes
Myths & Witches, Puzzles & Politics

BIBLIOGRAPHY

AA:	Secret Britain
William Cole:	Blecheley Diary
C. F. Farrar:	Ouse's Silent Tide
Hyde & Markham:	A History of Stony Stratford
Tony Ireson:	Northamptonshire
Ernest Reynolds:	Northamptonshire Treasures
E. S. Roscoe:	Buckinghamshire
Browne Willis:	History of Buckingham

PHOTOGRAPHS with the initials NK are by Norman Kent. Those with the initials JH are by the author

LIST OF ILLUSTRATIONS

Chapter 1

ODDLY ENOUGH

The National Lottery

National Lotteries were in the news in the 18th century. In 1766 William Cole, the Rector of St. Mary's Church in Bletchley, wrote in his diary:

> *'Sept. 1766. Wedn. 17. Windy. I called on Mr Cartwright before he went off, and gave him 10 Guineas to buy me a Lottery Ticker.'*

Mr Cartwright, who was the Roads Surveyor in Bletchley and often travelled to London, duly did as he was asked.

> *'Thursd. Oct.9. Excessive Cold and East Wind.*
> *Mr Natl. Cartwright came from London last night and brought me a Lottery Ticket No:14 m o 61 which cost £11 14s 6d., with the 6d for registering it.'*

The Rector carefully copied the ticket on the fly leaf of the Diary:

> *'Lottery*
> *Anno 1766   No: 14 m o 61*
> *The Ticket will entitle the Bearer thereof to six pounds or to a better chance in Annuities at the Rate of Three Pounds per Centum established by an Act of Parliament made in the sixth year of his Majesty's Reign, and transferable at the Bank of England.*
> *   J. White.'*

The Rector evidently missed out on any Prize in the Lottery and cut his losses. His Diary records:
'1766 Dec. Sund. 21. St. Thomas. Cold but fine Day. Mr Ja. Cartwright went to London and I gave him my Lottery Ticket to sell.'

So Cole got back £6 of the 10 Guineas he had invested.

❖ ❖ ❖ ❖ ❖

William Cole, 18th century Bletchley Rector and Diarist.

Gange Days

In May 1766 William Cole, the Bletchley Rector and Diarist, was in some discomfort:
> *'Saturday 3. Cold and Rainy. My knee where it was strained, uneasy. I had it pumped upon at the Pump in the Yard.'*

He managed to fulfil his duties at Church next day (Matins and Vespers). But on the Monday he was unable to join his parishioners on foot in Beating the Bounds of the Parish:
> *'Monday 5. Fine Day but windy. I went to meet my Parishioners who had been the Rounds of the Parish in procession, at the Corner of Rickley Wood. It being so windy, and the roads so bad for a Chaise, I did not care to go the whole way.'*

The three days before Holy Thursday were known in Buckinghamshire as 'Gange Days' and were marked by the walking of the parish boundaries. At Edgcott in Bucks., there was an acre of land called 'Gang Monday Land'. It was let at £3 per year and the money was used by the parish officers to provide cakes and ale for the occasion of Beating the Bounds. Clifton Reynes and Husborne Crawley made similar provisions.

Tin Can Band

At Broughton in Northamptonshire there is an ancient tradition observed at midnight on the second Sunday after St. Andrew's Day. People walk through the streets of Broughton banging on tin cans and buckets. The custom has been observed since the Middle Ages and was said to have been started 'to drive out gypsies'.

An attempt was made in 1929 to ban the custom but the Broughton folk were not to be denied. The authorities did their best, taking some of the offenders to court. But the custom survived, and still does. Even in the war years, when it was mutually agreed to forego the custom while the war was still on, it was still observed in token fashion. One man made the rounds, gently tapping his tin.

Mushie

In his working life, Mushie was part of a Circus Act. He was a fine Abyssinian lion. When his working days were over he lived 'in retirement' in Oundle, occupying a wheeled den next to his owner's caravan. Early most mornings he was taken out for a walk round the meadows. Oundle people took him in their stride, but he must have startled any visitors who suddenly came face-to-face with him.

Mushie always sensed when it was going to rain, and he used to give a mighty roar. 'Good as a barometer', Oundle folk said. In his old age, 13 or more, Mushie suffered from arthritis and there came a day when it was thought right to end his pain. So the Vet was called in, and Mushie was no more. They still have his skull in the Bio. Lab. at Kettering Grammar School.

The Unexpected Cave

In 1742 workmen were digging a hole in Royston in Herts. The ground gave way and they found themselves staring into a cave. That was surprise enough, but astonishment grew when it was found that the walls of the unexpected cave were adorned with works of art carved in the chalk rock. They could be called 'primitive art' but their subject matter was instantly recognisable – all the carvings were religious representations. The most obvious was clearly the Crucifixion. But study of two others showed them to be St. Catherine with her traditional wheel of torture, and St. Laurence. Other signs and symbols can also be been but are hard to identify.

The mystery is two-fold – when were these carvings made, and by whom? Could they date back to Anglo-Saxon times? Or

Strange chalk carvings discovered at Royston.

4

were they the work of the Knights Templar? Was the cave a very early hermitage – or an oratory – or a hiding place?

Perhaps the Knights Templar attribution is the most likely. The Knights Templar Order was founded in 1119 to protect pilgrims going to the Holy Land. The Order spread rapidly throughout Europe, but fell into disfavour in 1312 when it was suppressed. The English house of the Order was originally at Holborn but later moved to the Temple (hence Knights Templar). It could be that the strange cave in Royston was of their making after they had fallen out of favour.

It is possible to visit the cave on certain summer weekend afternoons on application to Royston Museum. The bell-shaped cave, beneath a busy street in the centre of Royston, is entered through a steep passage from the street.

Whit Monday 2002
This will be the date of the next Poll or Pole Fair in Corby. That is because it only happens every twenty years and the last one was on Whit Monday 1982. Why only every twenty years? Nobody knows.

What is known is that Elizabeth I granted to the then tiny hamlet of Corby a Charter to hold a Fair. Tradition says that the Queen awarded the Charter in appreciation of some Corby men having rescued her when she was thrown from her horse into a bog in Rockingham Forest. The Charter was later confirmed by Charles II.

Each time the 20th anniversary comes round, the Rector and Chairman of the local Council read the words of the Charter publicly. All roads leading into Corby are then closed off by gates. Visitors are only allowed through on payment of a small Toll. They can refuse to pay if they wish. But in that case they are liable to be taken to the stocks!

At Rothwell in Northants. they don't wait 20 years to hold *their* Fair. The Rothwell Fair happens every year and is one of the largest traditional Fairs in the county. It happens on the Monday after Trinity Sunday each year and starts at 6am. At that hour the Agent of the Lord of the Manor rides on horseback from the Manor House to the Market, accompanied by musicians and halberdiers. He reads out the Proclamation, and yet another Rothwell Fair opens.

❖ ❖ ❖ ❖ ❖

The Elephant Man

This true story begins in the East End of London and ends at Fawsley in Northants. It concerns a youth called John Merrick who, in the 1880s, was exhibited in the Mile End Road as a freak. People paid a shilling a time to see him. He was horribly deformed, and was so monstrous a sight that many fainted when his 'owner' drew back the curtain to reveal him.

He had an enormous mis-shapen head from which a bony tusk protruded. His deformed mouth prevented him from normal speech. Both his legs and one arm were grotesquely swollen and unwieldy. Yet his other arm was normal and ended in a delicate hand.

The Police closed down the 'peep show' and Merrick's minder took him to Belgium. But there too the exhibition was banned. The Elephant Man's minder then abandoned him in London. At this point Lady Knightly of Fawsley came to his rescue. She arranged for him to be taken to Fawsley and there a home was found for him in the cottage of a gamekeeper and his wife.

Despite his deformities and difficulty in speaking, John Merrick was far from being an imbecile. He was perfectly sane, but all too conscious of his revolting appearance. In the Northants. countryside he found peace and solitude, though only for a few months. He died in his bed, his neck dislocated by the enormous weight of his great head.

❖ ❖ ❖ ❖ ❖

'A Prodigy in Nature'

Stamford is at the meeting point of the counties of Leicestershire, Northants., and Huntingdonshire. At one end of the bridge over the Welland is Stamford-in-Northamptonshire. Here died in 1809 one Daniel Lambert – a 'Prodigy in Nature'.

His father kept Leicester Prison. As a youth Daniel was normal in every way. But at 19 he began to put on weight. That is putting it mildly – in no time at all he weighed 32 stone! His weight increased so alarmingly that he could no longer follow in his father's footsteps as a prison warder.

His weight went up to 52 stone! This wasn't because he ate

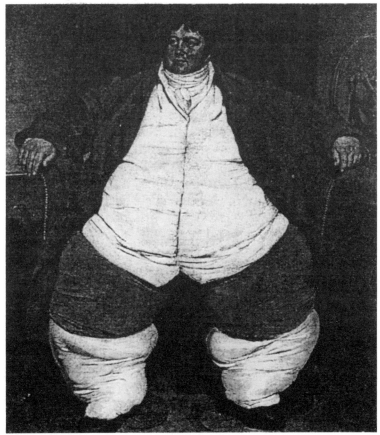

Daniel Lambert, 'a Prodigy in Nature' at 52 stone.

or drank excessively – he ate sparingly and drank only water. He wasn't slothful either – he was keenly interested in field sports, including fishing.

He decided to cash in on his huge size and ever-increasing weight. He went on tour as a one-man exhibition. And so it came about that on June 20th 1809 he arrived in Stamford – in time to put on his one-man show at the Race Meeting.

He lodged at the Waggon and Horses and went to bed at his usual time. And in the night he died. His funeral was phenomenal, not only for the crowds it attracted, but also for its logistics.

His coffin was gigantic – it had to be! It was an elm casket and a special 'hearse' had to be made to carry it. This extraordinary coffin was 6ft 4ins long, 4ft 4ins wide, and 2ft 4ins deep. It was mounted on two axle trees and four wheels. This meant that the coffin did not have to be lifted into any conventional hearse.

At the graveyard a long sloping channel ran down into the grave. Even so, it required nearly half an hour's exertion from over a hundred men to manoeuvre the coffin into the grave.

In due time a slate gravestone was put in place. Its wording paid due tribute to the extraordinary man it commemorates:

ALTUS IN ANIMO, IN CORPORE MAXIMUS
In Remembrance of that Prodigy in Nature
Daniel Lambert, a Native of Leicester,
Who was possessed of an Exalted and Convivial Mind
And in Personal Greatness had no Competitor
He measured 3ft 1in round the Leg
9ft 4ins round the Body,
and weighed 52 stone 11 lb
He departed this life on 21st June 1809 aged 39 years.
As a Testimony of Respect
This Stone is erected by his friends in Leicester.

Chapter 2

THE HAYSTACK THAT WASN'T

High up on the Dunstable Downs in World War II there stood a small isolated building. It was little more than a hut really, but it was cunningly disguised to look like a haystack. It was a very closely guarded secret and it housed an outstanding invention of British scientists.

Technically, that small building disguised as a haystack, was part of the Thunderstorm Location Unit of the Meteorological Office. There were four of these in Britain. Apart from the one on Dunstable Downs the other three were in Scotland, Northern Ireland, and Cornwall. Each of them could record simultaneously all the main lightning flashes within a radius of up to 2,000 miles.

All four units were linked electronically, and all four took soundings right round the clock. The little control station on Dunstable Downs would then plot all four bearings as lines on a map. In that way the exact location of thunderstorms could be pinpointed over an incredible radius of up to 2,000 miles. Updated forecasts were produced right round the clock, day and night.

That was vitally important in wartime. Icing on the wings of aircraft was almost as big a threat as anti-aircraft fire. Accurate forecasts could also tell whether bombing targets were likely to be obscured by thick clouds, and whether electrical disturbance would upset pilots' instruments.

It was claimed that the inventions used in those Thunderstorm Location Units saved hundreds of pilots' lives. The information gathered could be instantly passed to about

Dunstable Downs. A disguised haystack here determined the date of the Normandy Landings.

500 airfields all over Britain. The information was also passed to the Russians who were then our allies.

Every message transmitted during the war had, of course, to be sent by cipher. This was done from the Forecasting Centre down in Dunstable at the foot of the Downs. It was done by hundreds of women, members of the WAAF, who had to work at high speed.

It was from the Bedfordshire Downs that the vital weather forecast for D-Day was issued in 1944. That forecast led General Eisenhower to postpone the invasion from June 5th to June 6th – a vital decision. If the invasion had been attempted on June 5th the result could have been disastrous. Postponing it for 24 hours just made the Normandy landings possible and led to the ultimate victory.

So that secret little building, disguised as a haystack high up on Dunstable Downs played a key role in determining the outcome of World War II. So perhaps it deserves a place of honour alongside Bletchley Park. In their different ways both places were crucial. The modest little hut, disguised as a haystack on Dunstable Downs should never be forgotten, but should take its place in the annals of British history.

Fire over England

The threat and danger of war inspired the setting up of that secret hut high on Dunstable Downs. In the same way, in earlier centuries, when war was threatened, the nation turned to its hilltops. The creation of a chain of beacons to warn of imminent enemy attacks has a very long history. Every schoolboy knows how the beacon fires were lit to warn the nation that the Spanish Armada was coming in 1588.

Ellesborough Beacon Hill, one of a chain. (JH)

But in fact the use of beacon fires goes much further back than that. From 1324 onwards the records show that regulations were issued that beacons must be erected on suitable high points.

By the time that Elizabeth I came to the throne the whole beacon system was constantly updated and improved. By the early 1570s, when the Spanish threat grew ever more apparent, the chain of beacon sites had become a very important part of the defence of the realm.

The chain of command ran from the crown to county level, through Lords-Lieutenant to High Constables of the Hundreds, and to Constables of the parishes. Wherever there was a commanding highpoint, there was to be a beacon, maintained and manned, so that across the land there would be inter-visible viewpoints from which the message of fire could rapidly be transmitted. As Housman wrote in 'A Shropshire Lad':

'From Clee to heaven the beacon burns,
The Shires have seen it plain,
From north and south the sign returns
And beacons burn again'.

Ivinghoe

At a height of some 820 feet, Ivinghoe Beacon was a notable link in that chain. From its commanding height a panorama of outstretching country extends from the wooded borders of Bedfordshire, across the Vale of Aylesbury to the distant heights of Ashendon and Brill.

The word beacon, of Teutonic origin, appears in 14th century ordinances as 'Beknes'. In times of danger watch was to be kept at every beacon by two or three trustworthy men, answerable to the Justices of the Peace. They were to be alert, both to watch for signals from other beacons, and also to guard against vandalism, hoaxes, and the activities of agents provocateur.

'The Watchers must take hede that they fier not ther
beacons unadvisedlie uppon any other fyres whatsoever,
in any place uppon the view'.

So, with several centuries separating them, the men who manned the disguised haystack on Dunstable Downs in World War II, and the men who guarded the nearby Ivinghoe Beacon in the 16th century, had much in common. Both were vital links in the defence of the realm.

In the same way too, the soldiers who used Church Towers as observation points in the Civil War of 1642–47 – as in the Brickhills for example – were the predecessors of the men and women of the Observer Corps in World War II.

Ivinghoe Beacon carried the warning of the Armada.

From Beacon fires in the 16th century, to the lonely Storm Location Units and the Observer Corps in the 20th century there runs a continuing thread. The task of them all was the same – 'Keep Watch'. The price of freedom is eternal vigilance.

Chapter 3

A QUESTION OF SPORT

The gesture made by two upright fingers comes in two forms. If you raise two fingers with the palm facing the person you are greeting, your gesture is friendly and encouraging. You are making the 'V for Victory' sign which Churchill made so famous in World War II.

But if you make the same gesture of two upright fingers, with the back of your hand towards the person you are greeting, your gesture is rude and threatening.

The distinction between the two is well understood. But not everyone knows the historic background for it. It all started in the reign of Henry V. In 1415 he won the great victory over the French at the Battle of Agincourt. He owed that victory to the prowess of the archers in his army. Their skill with the longbow struck fear into the enemy. So much so that if an English bowman was captured in battle his captors took care to cut off two fingers of his right hand, so that never again could he practice his skill with the longbow in any future battle. Knowing this, the English bowman took to making the gesture of raising the two intact fingers to let the enemy know that he could still use his longbow with deadly effect.

In archery the English had a most effective weapon. But it needed practice. There had been a time in English history when skill with the bow had declined. Alarmed at this, the King in 1389 had passed an Act. 'Cause public proclamation', it said, 'that the people at leisure times and on holidays use in their recreation bows and arrows'. To foster archery handball and football were forbidden under pain of imprisonment. All other sports save archery were forbidden on Sundays and Feastdays. It was also decreed that if an archer killed a man while practising, the misadventure should not be considered a crime.

Longbow men practising at the archery butts. (Luttrell Psalter c1340).

Throughout the country men were encouraged to practice archery in churchyards and on village greens. The Lord of the Manor of Willington in Bedfordshire used his authority to decree that no-one must play at tennis until twelve years old, and only then at Christmas. And the men should get their amusement by practising archery.

The policy paid off, as the victory of Agincourt demonstrated. Much later in our history Wellington was to say: 'The Battle of Waterloo was won on the playing fields of Eton'. The Battle of Agincourt could equally be said to have been won at the Archery Butts on village greens all over the country. Long after Agincourt the importance of archery continued to be recognised. In 1469 in Leighton Buzzard tennis, quoits and dice were forbidden in the hope that men would spend their leisure practising archery.

Other warlike skills were also developed in sporting pastimes. Fighting with broadswords and quarterstaff, for example. And, higher up the social scale, tournaments were much in vogue from the 12th century onwards. They provided the opportunity in 'mimic warfare' for young knights to display their strength and prowess.

Both Bedford and Dunstable were popular venues for tournaments. Dunstable, because of its accessibility on the

Watling Street, was much favoured by royalty for tournaments. Edward III twice attended tournaments there.

But tournaments, attracting the nobility, could also be occasions for plotting. With the growing resentment against the king felt by many barons, tournaments were banned at Dunstable in 1250 and at Bedford in 1255. But that was only a temporary interruption – tournaments were certainly held again at Dunstable in 1308 and 1334.

For ordinary folk, not directly involved in tournaments, there was no lack of sporting activity. Bowls were very popular. Dunstable's bowling alley was leased in 1624 for 6s 6d per year. Village bowling alleys existed in the 17th century in many places. They are mentioned in Clophill, Harrold, Renhold and Toddington. And great landowners had their own bowling greens at their stately homes. Lord Bolingbroke had one. So, too, did the Duke of Bedford at Woburn.

When Celia Fiennes made her epic journeys on horseback all over England in the 1680s she visited Woburn. In her diary she wrote:

> *'Thence to Ouburn, the Duke of Bedford's house which stands in a fine parke full of deer . . . the gardens are fine . . . there is a large bowling green with 8 arbours kept neately, and seats in each'.*

She visited Bedford too and liked it very much. Her diary describes the river and its amenities:

> *'It runns by a ground which is made into a fine bowling green; it is well kept with seates and summer houses in it for the use of Town and Country gentlemen of which many resort to it especially the Market dayes'.*

Football had its devotees also. It originated as a game for the open streets, but it came in time to be played in a close. Colmworth, Eaton Socon and Felmersham all had such pitches.

Cricket traces its origins to Hambledon in Hampshire in the early 1730s. The first literary reference to the game in North Bucks. is found in the diary of William Cole, the Rector of Bletchley. He records that in 1766 his handyman, Tom, together with servants from the house of Browne Willis, the Lord of the Manor, went to a cricket match at Stony Stratford.

Before long virtually every large village had its own cricket team. Mostly the pitch would be the village green. This was the case at Deanshanger. But there was an outrage there in 1815 when John Clarke, the local landowner, tried to enclose the green. As fast as he erected fences, the villagers pulled them down. Confrontation between villagers and landowner grew fierce.

There came a day when the villagers decided to hold a 'Play in'. They assembled on the green and proceeded to play not only cricket, but a game of football as well! In this they were much encouraged by Lord Charles Fitzroy. While play went on two solicitors rode round the green on their horses.

John Clarke was frustrated, but he was determined to get his way. In 1836 he brought a case at the Stony Stratford Quarter Sessions against six Deanshanger men for 'malicious destruction of herbage of the Green by playing at cricket'. The Magistrates, including the sporting parson, the Reverend Loraine-Smith, Rector of Passenham, threw out the case. The villagers had won. That night 'seventy people played games on the Green'.

Cricket also had its devotees among the aristocracy. The 4th Duke of Bedford was an enthusiast and matches were played regularly at Woburn. One notable game was played there in 1757 between a team captained by Lord Sandwich and a team led by Mr St. John. The game was 'won hollow' by the latter.

At Biggleswade cricket matches were played on the common. A match played there in 1829 was won by Biggleswade Juniors (under 20). They beat Potton by 111 runs to 77. At Luton a marquee was erected to serve as a pavilion. There was great anger in 1822 when the players' clothes were stolen from the marquee during a match.

Other far less attractive 'sports' had their followings too. Bull-baiting and bear-baiting used to take place in St. Paul's Churchyard in Bedford. There was bear-baiting at Woburn Church in 1612.

Cockfighting took place at Knotting Church in the 1630s. It took place regularly on Shrove Tuesday with the connivance of the Churchwardens. Ampthill was no better. Cockfighting took place there on Boxing Day in 1680. A man named John Newland, needing money to wager on the cockfighting, broke into a house on Christmas Day while the family were at church, and stole £6 from a chest.

Boxing in the form of prize fighting was illegal but went on in spite of the ban. The Justices of the Peace declared them unlawful because they were 'convinced of their ill tendency'. They declared themselves 'determined not to suffer them to take place'. But the public could be equally determined. Even though the Quarter Sessions dealt severely with those who organised, took part in, or even attended a Prize Fight, such fights still took place. Their venues of course had to be kept secret, and often there was a battle of wits between the 'Fancy', as the supporters and patrons of boxing were called, and the police.

A famous, or notorious, Prize Fight took place in 1845 on the Biddenham side of Bedford. The contestants were Robert Goddard and Charles Johnson. The Police, who had done their homework, thought they knew where the fight was to take place. But the organisers were too smart for them. They had a fall-back plan and at the last minute they switched the venue to Fenlake on the other side of the river. There, about one thousand spectators gathered to watch the fight. The wrong-footed police were fuming on the wrong side of the river and had no boats to get them across. The fight lasted for 42 bloody rounds. Goddard won, and the battered Johnson was carried off to hospital.

There had earlier been a similar Prize Fight at Hanslope in 1830 between McKay, a famous Scottish prize fighter, and an Irishman, Simon Byrne. The fight ended after 47 rounds when

Prize Fighting – illegal but popular.

McKay could no longer continue. He was carried unconscious to the inn where he died. He was buried in Hanslope Churchyard. The epitaph on his tombstone ends with the couplet:

> *'If you have ever fought before*
> *Take my advice and fight no more'.*

It is not clear whether we are to take this warning as being given either *to* McKay, or *by* McKay. In any case McKay was never to fight again for his last fight had killed him.

Croquet, billiards, golf, tennis – all these are still with us. They have a long history. The South Bedfordshire Croquet Club was established in 1871. The Earl of Cleveland's house at Toddington had a billiard table in 1644. Twelve men were fined 20d each at Ampthill in 1502 for playing tennis when they should have been practising archery.

Sports and pastimes are part of a nation's history. They give pleasure to those who practise them and to spectators. They can bring tangible rewards too – prizes to winning contestants and profits to the punters who back the winners. And there is also the accolade of being CHAMPION!

Perhaps it comes as no surprise that the British love of sports, and its praise for champions is reflected in the ancient tradition of the Champion of England, or King's Champion.

Originally the King's Champion was the official whose duty it was to ride into Westminster Hall and to challenge anyone who might be tempted to dispute the right of succession of the new monarch. It was William the Conqueror, no less, who initiated this office. Its first holder was Robert de Marmion and the intention was that the duty should be passed on to his male descendants. With the appointment went also the manor of Scrivelsby. By the reign of Richard II, Sir John Symoke held the Manor and its attendant duties. The last monarch to see the custom of the King's Champion, carried out in its original form was George IV. Today the office of King's Champion still survives though nowadays it is confined to the right to carry the sovereign's standard at the coronation.

A serious 'question of sport' has already been answered in a number of pastimes. Dog fights are illegal; Hare-coursing is banned; Bull and Bear baiting are forbidden; Badger hunting is prohibited, as is Cockfighting. It may be that other sports in the future will get the red card. But it is unthinkable that sport will ever disappear – it is too deeply rooted in the human psyche.

Chapter 4

MIND YOUR MANORS !

Bacon once wrote: 'Houses are built to live in; therefore let use be preferred before uniformity, except where both may be had'.

From the 14th century onwards a great multiplication of manor houses occurred. By 1400 there were already about fifty of them in Bedfordshire for example. That number rose rapidly till by the 15th century there were over four hundred.

They were not fortified. They were the homes of the gentry, the barons and knights. They farmed the land, or had it farmed for them, and beyond that they lived on their rents. From time to time their ranks were swollen by the arrival of business men from London – often members of one or other of the City Guilds or Companies, who acquired manors in the country.

Judicious marriages united one manor with another, and so the quality and status of manor houses grew.

Most influential of all was the effect of the dissolution of monastic houses at the Reformation. For then the great monastic land-holdings were broken up, and some of the wealth (and precious building materials) filtered down to lay land-owners and barons and knights. This in time led to the upgrading of many manor houses into something far grander. So grew many of the stately homes we know today.

It so happens that lying within five miles of each other in the valley of the Ouse there is a quartet of great houses each of whose stories can be traced from Manor House to stately home. Their location in the Great Ouse Valley is not the only factor that links them. They also have in common the fact that they are all in North Bucks., and they all have roots going back to the

*Berkhamsted motte and baily castle, one of 250 built by the Conqueror.
Many later became Manors.*

Domesday Survey. They are: Gayhurst, Tyringham, Great
Linford, and Chicheley.

Their actual buildings date back only to Jacobean times. But
all four of them were built on the site, and incorporated the
foundations of, much earlier buildings.

All four of them are examples of remarkable continuity.
Gayhurst passed by direct lineal descent or by marriage in the
same family from the 12th to the 17th century. Tyringham
remained in one family also from the 12th to the 17th century.
At Chicheley the Chester line runs from the 16th to the 20th
century. At Great Linford the Utthwatt family lived in the
Manor House from 1704 until the 1960s.

With the Manors there were, and there still are, the
churches. The house of God is historically found alongside the
house of the Lord of the Manor. And in the churches the
continuity is even more impressive. The lists of Rectors in the
churches associated with these four great houses are complete

from the 13th century right up to the present day.

Advowson, the right of presentation to a vacant benefice, historically belonged to the Lord of the Manor. This right was highly valued and for the most part, it was conscientiously exercised. Nowadays the patronage of livings has often passed to the diocesan authorities.

Gayhurst

At the Conquest this Manor was one of many awarded to Odo, Bishop of Bayeux, the Conqueror's brother. He passed it on to the Bishop of Lisieux, who in his turn installed Robert de Noyer.

Odo lost all his Manors when, after the death of William the Conqueror, he supported the claim to the throne of Robert, the Conqueror's first-born son. Robert's claim failed, and Odo, and all others who had supported his cause, were stripped of their possessions. Oddly, however, Gayhurst was not forfeited to the

Gayhurst Manor – secret passages and a priest's hiding place. (NK)

new king, William (Rufus) II. Instead it was allowed to remain in the hands of Robert de Noyer. The de Noyer family held Gayhurst from 1086 to 1396, when the last male de Noyer died. At that point Joan de Noyer married Sir Robert Nevill and Gayhurst was held by the Nevill family until 1581 when the last male Nevill died.

That date, 1581, proved a climactic date for Gayhurst. Mary, the sister of the last male Nevill, was married twice – first to William Mulsho to whom she bore a son, also named William. On her husband's death she was married again, to Christopher Slingsby. No children were born to that second marriage and the Slingsby family made a settlement of the estate in favour of William Mulsho.

But to prevent any question of title arising, Elizabeth I granted a patent conferring the Manor on Sir Francis Drake. That patent was dated 13 January, 1581. The following day, 14 January, 1581, Sir Francis Drake sold the reversion to William Mulsho. So the Mulsho title to the property was secured.

The Manor House then was fairly modest. It had been built about 1520. William Mulsho set to work to enlarge it. He died on 20 October 1601, and his only child, Mary, succeeded him. She had married in 1596 and her husband took over the completion of the building. That husband was the man whose name will be forever remembered as linking Gayhurst to the Gunpowder Plot. He was Sir Everard Digby.

Sir Francis Drake. He owned Gayhurst but only for one day.

Everard Digby came of ancient stock, tracing his lineage back to the 11th century. He had been born in the climactic year, 1581, and in April 1603 he had been knighted by the new king, James I.

Everard Digby was a devout catholic. He was well placed, therefore, in his completion of the building of Gayhurst to include in the enlarged building both a secret chapel high up under the roof, and elsewhere in the house a priest's hiding place and a number of secret passages. So Mass could be said and a priest to celebrate it could be safely housed.

Catholic priests were not the only secret visitors. There also came Guy Fawkes and Robert Catesby. At Gayhurst, and also at Ashby Ledger in Northamptonshire, the Gunpowder Plot was hatched. It was intended to blow up not only Parliament, but also the king and members of his family.

But it all went horribly wrong. The plot was betrayed and Guy Fawkes was caught red-handed just as he was preparing to ignite the fuse to detonate the thirty-six barrels of gunpowder assembled in the cellar beneath Parliament. The date was November 5th, 1605.

All the plotters were put to death and it might have been expected that the Gayhurst estate would be confiscated by the crown. But this did not happen because the house was vested in the name of Everard Digby's wife. So she was able to continue to live there and to bring up her two young sons. Both sons grew to manhood, both were knighted, and both served their nation and monarch in the Civil War.

Gayhurst remained in the Digby hands until 1704 when the estate was sold for £27,000 to George Wrighte, the son of Sir Nathan Wrighte, Lord Keeper of the Great Seal.

In the 19th century Gayhurst was let to Lord Carrington on a twenty-one year repairing lease. Unfortunately Lord Carrington blocked up virtually all the secret passages and the secret priest's room.

In the past hundred years Gayhurst has changed hands several times. Twice it became a school. And in World War II it became a satellite to Bletchley Park engaged in under-cover war work.

So Gayhurst, as a Manor, has existed for a thousand years. It began in the days of the last Saxon kings. It continued through the reigns of forty monarchs – Norman, Plantagenet, Lancastrian, Yorkist, Tudor, Hanoverian, Saxe-Coburg, and Windsor. It survived the eleven years of the Commonwealth under Cromwell. In one way or another it was involved in the 17th century Civil War and in the two World Wars of the 20th century.

Today it remains a lovely building. Now in private hands, it is divided into a number of gracious apartments.

Tyringham

Less than three miles from Gayhurst, on the other side of the River Ouse, stands Tyringham. It was a Manor in Saxon hands until the Conquest when it was granted to Geoffrey, Bishop of Coutance. He was also given the Manors of Water Eaton, Bletchley, Fenny Stratford and Simpson, as well as extensive lands in the west country. But, like Bishop Odo, he lost the lot because he backed the wrong side in the rebellion led by Robert, the first-born son of William I. Tyringham was then given to William Fitz-Ausculf who installed Acard as his tenant.

A great-grandson of Acard was Giffard de Tyringham and he it was who began the long Tyringham family succession which lasted for the next six hundred years.

One of the Tyringhams was beheaded following the Battle of Wakefield in 1461 in the Wars of the Roses. In the Civil War in the 17th century also members of the Tyringham family lost their lives, fighting for the King.

A kinsman by marriage of the Tyringham family was Robert Catesby of Ashby Ledger. He was a Catholic and a close friend of Everard Digby of Gayhurst. He became a co-conspirator with Guy Fawkes and Everard Digby in the abortive Gunpowder Plot and, like them, paid for it with his life.

The Tyringham Estate comprised about 1,750 acres. The Manor House over the years had been enlarged and improved.

Tyringham Manor remained with one family for five centuries. (JH)

It was described both by Lipscomb and by Cole, the Bletchley Rector and Diarist, as being an excellent building of noble proportions.

In the 17th century the Tyringham family became extinct in the male line. The Manor was left to Elizabeth Tyringham who married John Backwell, as Alderman of London. They had many children. Their first-born son was baptised with the name Tyringham and this custom was followed for the next three generations.

By the middle of the 18th century the Tyringham-Backwell family became extinct in the male line and the Manor was inherited by Elizabeth Backwell. She too married a Londoner, William Praed. In 1859 he dropped the Praed name and assumed the Tyringham name.

William Praed in 1792 pulled down the Tyringham Manor House and built in its place the present mansion. He employed John Soane, a young architect who later went on to fame and fortune as the designer of the Bank of England.

In 1906 the banker Frederick Adolphus Konig bought the

27

estate. He made extensive alterations. He employed Lutyens to design splendid new features in the grounds, including extensive pools and ornate pavilions. Lutyens later found fame as the designer of the Cenotaph in Whitehall and as the Chief Architect of New Delhi.

Konig died in 1940 but his widow survived until 1951. During World War II Tyringham became a Maternity Hospital for evacuees. After the war it was bought by the Australia and New Zealand Bank and was used as a weekend Club House. In May 1967 Tyringham House was bought by a Trust Fund headed by Sir Maurice Laing and the present Tyringham Naturopathic Clinic was opened.

Great Linford

Unlike Gayhurst and Tyringham, which were in the Bonestou Hundred, Great Linford was in the Sigelei Hundred. This Hundred was almost exactly coterminous in acreage with the new city of Milton Keynes. Great Linford Manor has been described as 'the only place approaching a stately home in the Milton Keynes city area'. This is remarkable when it is recalled

Great Linford Manor. Its origins predate the Conquest by more than a century. (JH)

that so many other Manors and great houses in this area are no more. The Manors of Water Eaton, Bletchley, Fenny Stratford, Simpson and Wolverton are all gone. Nothing remains of the great houses of the Giffords, the Longuevilles, Browne Willis and the rest. But Great Linford survives.

It has another claim to fame too. Its first recorded appearance dates back more than a century before the Conquest. King Edmund in 944 gave it to his thegn Aelfheah.

At the Conquest part of the Great Linford lands were given to the Earl of Morton, and part was given to Hugh de Bolebec. When the latter died the two halves came together as a single Manor. It was Hugh de Bolebec who founded Woburn Abbey.

After Hugh de Bolebec died Great Linford changed hands many times. For a brief period it was owned by Sir Anthony Tyringham. In 1462 Great Linford was granted to Richard Middleton (which is why we have Middleton Hall in the MK City Centre).

There had been a quite large medieval hall-house at Great Linford, but when Sir William Pritchard bought the estate in 1682 he rebuilt the Manor House on a new site, using material from the former building. He also built the Pavilions and the Barn, and the attractive row of Almshouses.

At the beginning of the 18th century the Utthwatt family acquired the property and continued in occupation right up to the 1960s. The Utthwatts enlarged and remodelled the Manor House.

Great Linford Manor House today is privately owned. But all the other Great Linford buildings have taken on a new lease of life. The Almshouses are now craft workshops; the two Pavilions and Barn now comprise the Courtyard, a complex serving as a centre for Arts and Crafts and as venue for community activities.

Chicheley

'The superbly proportioned and perfectly symmetrical Chicheley Hall' was built in 1701 for Sir John Chester. But Chicheley's history stretches back for a thousand years before

that. It figured in Domesday not as one Manor, but as three –
Tickford, Chicheley, and Thickthorne, all owned by William
Fitz-Ausculf.

As a single Manor in the 12th century it descended to Fulk
Pagenell. He founded Tickford Priory on which he bestowed
Chicheley land. Tickford Priory retained its interest in
Chicheley right up to 1526 when, in common with all other
Religious Houses, it was dissolved.

In 1546 Henry VIII bestowed Chicheley Manor on Anthony
Cave, a wealthy wool merchant. He built a new Manor House
at Chicheley, but nothing remains of that Tudor House save
some traces of its foundations.

Anthony Cave died in 1558 leaving no male heir. His
daughter, Judith, married William Chester, member of a
wealthy London family. Chicheley was to remain in the Chester
family right up to the 20th century.

Sir Anthony was an ardent Royalist in the Civil War and
fought at the Battle of Naseby. After that battle the Royalist
cause was lost. In 1646 Chicheley Hall was plundered and
sacked by Parliamentary troops. Sir Anthony fled to Holland

Chicheley— 'Superbly proportioned and perfectly symmetrical'. (JH)

where he remained in exile until 1650.

For the next generation the Chester family was heavily encumbered., But a successful marriage restored the family fortune somewhat.

Anthony's second son, Sir John Chester, built the present Chicheley Hall. It took four years to build and used a million bricks. The house remained with the Chesters till 1952, when it was bought by the second Earl Beatty, son of the famous World War I Admiral. Admiral Beatty died in 1936 and was buried in St. Pauls' Cathedral. His son, having bought Chicheley Hall in 1952, brought together in the house many works of marine art and Beatty memorabilia. He died in 1972 and Chicheley Hall today is the home of his son, Nicholas Beatty.

Chapter 5

SUMMONED BY BELLS

'I heard the church bells hollowing out the sky,
Deep beyond deep, like never-ending stars'.

So wrote Sir John Betjeman in his blank-verse autobiography. He was Poet Laureate in the 1970s. Bells exercise an endless fascination.

At Guilsborough in Northamptonshire there are inscriptions on the church bells claiming that the ringing of them wards off plagues. At Weedon Lois in the same county it was claimed that the bells averted thunder.

In many places the tolling of the Passing Bell after a death was thought to drive away demons. In England the tradition has long been that to protect a passing soul, 'tellers' are tolled – nine for a man, six for a women. In both cases the bell is then further tolled for the number of times equal to the age of the deceased, one strike for each year of life.

At Ayot St. Peter in Hertfordshire it is the custom that every Good Friday the 'Nine Tailors' are rung, followed by the tolling thirty-three more times to signify the age of our Lord at His Crucifixion. The 'Nine Tailors' is a corruption of the word 'tellers', a 'teller' being a strike of the funeral bell.

At Mardon, also in Hertfordshire, a bell was found in a pond in 1848. Some said that the bell had fallen into the hands of a mermaid centuries before. It was directed that the bell should be recovered from the pond, but that great care should be taken in the operation. It was to be drawn from the water in silence, by white heifers decked with yew and mountain ash.

On the appointed day all went well, until an excited driver made a noise. Immediately the mermaid snatched the bell back again and it could be heard ringing in the water. However, the operation was later accomplished successfully, and the bell is now safely on dry land.

There was a much less satisfactory outcome in the 17th century at Chidlington. This village is near the Hertfordshire border. What happened there was described in 'The Englishman's Leisure in the 17th century' – an example of the indignation and intervention of God following a case of gross desecration. The account relates:

'At Chidlington upon the edge of Hertfordshire, not farre from Hitchin, a company of fellowes upon a holy day being to play a match, at foot ball, one of them was tolling the bell, to

The 'Mermaid Bell' at Mardon.

assemble the rest, some being come into the church the rendevoze of their meeting, suddainly it thundering was seene a blacke ball came tumbling downe a hill neere by; which tooke its course directly into the Church, there it flew into the bell-free and first slew him that tolled the bell, then it flustered about the Church and hurted divers of them, and at last bursting; left a filthy stinnke like to that of brimstone and so left a terror to all such spend-thrifts of precious time, and especially such as is dedicated to sacred uses. Who so is wise and will observe these things, even they shall understand the loving kindness of the Lord'.

During World War II Churchill decreed that Church bells should not be rung, except as a warning should the Germans invade. Happily they didn't, so, even more happily, the bells did ring again to celebrate the victory when it came.

Exactly two hundred years before World War II began, England had entered another war. That was in 1739 and the war was with Spain. The Spanish greeted the war with peals of bells. This prompted Robert Walpole, Churchill's predecessor as Prime Minister, to say; 'They now ring the bells, but they will soon wring their hands'.

English bell ringing is deservedly famous. The art of campanology is called Change Ringing. To discover how many changes can be rung on a peal, you have to multiply the number of bells in the peal by the number of changes that can be rung on a peal, consisting of one bell less. Confused? Well, 1 bell, no change; 2 bells, 1 by 2 = 2 changes; 3 bells, 2 by 3 = 6 changes; 4 bells, 6 x 4 = 24 changes; 5 bells, 24 x 5 = 120 changes; 6 bells, 120 x 6 = 720 changes.

Bow Brickhill Church. (NK)

Still confused? Never mind. Just enjoy the bells. And marvel at the skill and dedication of the ringers who can take several hours to ring Grandshire Triples and similar tours-de-force.

And admire, too, the ingenuity of Mr Goode who called the faithful to worship at Bow Brickhill Church for more than forty years. He tolled three bells, not only single-handedly but also single-footedly. He tolled two of the bells with his left and right hands, and the third bells he tolled by one foot in a loop at the end of the third bell rope.

Mr Goode bell-ringing at Bow Brickhill with two hands and one leg. (JH).

Chapter 6

CLERICAL ERRORS

Thomas Stafford, Lord of Tattenhoe Manor, was not married. But he did have an illegitimate son, named William. He loved his son dearly and when he died in 1515 he left his Manor to the lad. And he did more than this. He left the sum of £10 to the Reverend Sir John Bentley, the Vicar of Mursley, so that the vicar could instruct the boy for three years 'in the seyence of grammar' and so prepare him to go up to the University. Thomas must have died content in the knowledge that he had provided handsomely for the boy.

However, it did not work out so smoothly. Thomas Stafford had a cousin who considered himself the rightful heir to the Tattenhoe property and objected strongly to the inheritance going to 'the bastard heir'. The angry cousin rejoiced in the rather splendid name of Sir Humphrey de Blatherwyke. Sir Humphrey managed to get hold of the Tattenhoe title deeds and sent them to Woburn Abbey for safe keeping. William, 'the bastard heir', was determined not to be deprived of his inheritance so he sued the Abbot of Woburn for the return of the title deeds. The action was only partly successful. The matter was resolved in such a way that William should have Tattenhoe Manor for his life time but that he should pay £10 rent for it to the legitimate Stafford heirs. Meanwhile the vicar of Mursley had no doubt earned his fees for teaching young William 'the seyence of grammar' though there is no evidence that the lad ever went to university.

❖ ❖ ❖ ❖ ❖

The Normans effected an enormous change in English church life. Many of the pre-Conquest cathedrals were moved to new centres and soon virtually all the bishops were Norman. There was a proliferation of new Guilds, Priories and Abbeys and the number of parish clergy greatly increased. But occasionally there were outbursts against individual priests.

One victim of this was Thomas Curteys, vicar of Great Brickhill. For some reason he occasioned the great wrath of William de Poleye. William seized the Reverend Thomas Curteys and carried him off to imprisonment in Snellerston Manor at Lavendon. William kept Thomas prisoner there until someone came up with the twelve marks ransom which William demanded. This little episode took place in 1276.

Half a century later, in 1334, it was the turn of the Reverend William Gryk to get into difficulties. He was the priest of one of the churches in Stony Stratford. He owned land of his own but trespassed on land which was not his, in Whittlewood Forest. He was arrested and imprisoned in Aylesbury for many months before his case was even heard. After more than a year he succeeded in getting bail. Eventually he was able to plead his case before the Justices of the Pleas of the Forest.

A Different Sort of Trespass

The Reverend William Gryk's offence had been trespassing. Three centuries later many Anglican clergy accused the Reverend John Wesley of trespass of a different kind because he felt free to go where he liked to preach the gospel. The Church of England at that time was not at its liveliest and Wesley, himself an Anglican priest, wanted to stir it up. So he 'trespassed', preaching tirelessly up and down the land until he was over eighty. 'It is

John Wesley visited Bedford thirty-two times to preach.

true,' he wrote in his diary, 'I travel four or five thousand miles in a year.'

In his seventy-first year he wrote: 'Preaching at five in the morning is one of the most healthy exercises in the world'. He visited Bedford thirty-two times to preach. Sometimes he found Bedford folk less than attentive! 'These drowsy people,' he once wrote, 'a more sleepy audience I have not often seen'. Even at seventy-three the programme he set himself would have daunted a much younger man.

'10 November 1776 Rode from Northampton to Luton. Preached at Luton and Sundon.
Tuesday 11 November Preached at Millbrook and Wrotten Pillinge.
Wednesday 12 November Preached Bedford'.

Wesley's Oak barely survives at Stony Stratford. (NK)

In his eighty-eighth year, five months before he died, Wesley preached for the last time in Bedford, 'held up in the pulpit by two ministers'.

Bedford had a notable evangelist of its own. He was the Reverend Timothy Matthews, Chaplain of Bedford's House of Industry early in the 19th century. His preaching drew enormous crowds and he averaged some six sermons a week in Bedford and the surrounding countryside.

He liked to blow his own trumpet, but this was no clerical error of sinful pride. He blew the trumpet to collect an audience. (They have it still in the Chapel at Ravensden.) For Matthews the Ouse was his Jordan and he loved to baptise converts there in the early morning. He had some reputation for faith healing. In 1845 he died of typhus and his final burying place was Colmforth where he had once been curate.

Milton described the age in which he lived, the 17th century, as 'the womb of teeming birth'. Church life then was a roller-coaster, veering from one extreme to another – High Church, Puritan, Protestant. Sects proliferated – Calvanist, Presbyterian, Baptist, Quaker, Millenarian. There were even the Ranters, the Seekers, and the Muggletonians! In such a kaleidoscope there was plenty of room for clerical error!

The Reverend Giles Thorne was made Rector of St. Peter and St. Paul in Bedford in 1629. He was attacked for 'not praying for the king'. Later in the century he would have been punished severely if he *had* prayed for the king!

Thorne was a High Churchman and was sent to the Fleet Prison in 1642 for what was considered his 'papalistic' teaching. Ironically, while he languished in the Fleet Prison news reached him that he had been appointed Archdeacon of Buckingham. But on the very same day the Puritan-minded Parliament was preparing to abolish Archbishops, Bishops, Deans, Canons – and Archdeacons!

Poor Thorne stayed in prison for five years. He was then

allowed out on bail but only for six weeks. In those strange times Parliament set up two Committees. One was 'The Committee of Plundered Ministers'. The other was 'The Committee of Scandalous Ministers'. Which of the two handled the case of Giles Thorne is not clear. He was finally released in 1646. All came right for him in the end. At the Restoration of Charles II he not only returned in triumph to his Rectory of St. Mary's at Bedford but he was also made Archdeacon of Buckingham after all! He died in 1671 and his tombstone bears the inscription:

'Underneath heare lyes Buried ye Bodie of Giles Thorne,
Doctor in Divinity, Chaplaine in Ordinary to King Charles
ye 2nd, Archdeacon of Buckingham, and Rector of St. Marie's
and St. Peter's heare in Bedford, who deceased June ye 23, 1671.'

Clerical error was sometimes seen not only individuals but in groups. Tickford Priory in Newport Pagnell provides an example. It had been founded by Fulk Paganell in 1140 and normally comprised some sixteen monks, all of French origin. The Priory became quite wealthy and acquired the churches and tithes of over a dozen parishes in the neighbourhood. With its French connections it was deemed an 'alien' Priory in the reigns of Edward III and Richard II, during the hundred years war with France, and its income was seized by the King.

But that was the least of its troubles. The fact is that the Priory was not well run. Its numbers were down and its monastic rule was badly kept. The Bishop of Lincoln castigated it for its laxity and ordered that it should mend its ways and recruit new members.

In 1275 Simon de Reda became Prior. This proved a disastrous appointment. By 1278 the Under Sheriff of Buckinghamshire, Reginald de Grey, seized the Priory in the King's name. He put in prison the monks 'who had lately been under the leadership of one who had been excommunicated for his excesses (meaning Simon de Reda) and had wasted the goods of the Monastery'.

But Simon de Reda was a hard man to put down. He contrived to hold on to his Priorship. The Bishop of Lincoln paid a second punitive visit in 1290, when his visit was physically resisted by the monks. But the bishop was adamant. Simon de Reda must go! And go he did, deposed in 1291 on the grave charges of 'waste of goods, evil living – and homicide!' Clerical error indeed!

You might suppose that Tickford Priory would behave itself after that. Not a bit of it. In 1340 virtually open warfare broke out between the monks and the Vicar and parishioners of Newport. The Prior and his monks besieged the vicarage, broke down the doors, smashed the windows, insulted the vicar, beating and wounding him, and carrying off some £10 worth of his goods.

Cardinal Wolsey had the last word. In 1524 he closed down the 'superfluous house of Tickford' and diverted all its income to the college, Christ Church, which he was founding in Oxford.

Perhaps Northamptonshire's contribution to this catalogue of clerical errors is best represented by some 16th century citizens of Oundle. One was Giles Wigginton and the other was William Hacket. Good Queen Bess was then on the throne, doing her best to find a 'middle way' between the extremes of Puritanism and Catholicism. The Archbishop was Whitgift who shared the Queen's dislike of religious extremes. So it is not surprising that Archbishop Whitgift disapproved of Wigginton who was a Puritan. He not only forbade him to preach, he also had him imprisoned.

Enter at this point William Hacket. He was a man of dissolute character who was convinced that he had a mission to take over the government not only of England but of the world. He made a start at York where he said he had come to announce the imminent arrival of the Messiah. He was chased out of the city, Next he tried Leicester where he was also expelled. And so to Northampton, where he was put in prison.

Enter next Edmund Coppinger, an obscure member of the Queen's household. When both Wigginton and Hacket were released from their respective prisons, Coppinger declared himself their ally. And under Hacket's leadership the trio relaunched the campaign to achieve world leadership. They loudly announced their manifesto, which was to:

> Remove Elizabeth from the throne
> Enthrone Hacket in her place, and
> Abolish all bishops.

Standing in a cart, drawn through the streets of London, they proclaimed their programme to huge crowds. Arrests followed and Hacket, blaspheming to the end, was executed. His was a costly clerical error if ever there was one!

❖ ❖ ❖ ❖ ❖

It is almost refreshing to leave such examples of 'clerical error' in earlier centuries and to turn instead to the story of the great sporting parson of Passenham. He was not only the Vicar of Passenham, he was also a Magistrate. And he was a sportsman with a great liking for prize fighting. In fact he was himself a great pugilist. He was the Reverend Loraine Smith and he lived about a hundred and fifty years ago. (For his sporting sympathies with the village cricketers against a rapacious landowner see page 17.)

Prize fighting was illegal. Despite this Loraine Smith himself helped to arrange some prize fights. Passenham being so close to the Bucks./Northants. border, it was easy to switch at the last minute from one side of the border to the other to avoid police harassment. But the conflict between his sporting instincts and his conscience as a Magistrate posed problems for the sporting parson. On one occasion he had been obliged, as a

Magistrate, to help the police organise a raid on an illegal prize fight. The police managed to stop the fight and the crowd scattered. But when the police tried to arrest one of the fighters he simply laid out the constables! It was then left to the Magistrate/Parson/Pugilist Loraine Smith to arrest the offender. But he let him go again with no more than a friendly caution.

The great 18th century clerical wit, the Reverend Sydney Smith, once said 'What a pity it is that we have no amusements in England but vice and religion'. It could be said, perhaps, that clerical errors often neatly combine the two.

Chapter 7

NOT FOR THE FIRST TIME

Legend says that Dunstable gets its name from a villain called
Dun. He led a gang of robbers far back in the mists of time, and
his notoriety found expression in the place name of the area
where he practised his villainy.

In 1690 the so-called St. Albans gang struck fear into the
hearts of the inhabitants of that historic city.

In the 1820s the notorious 'Captain Slash' led his gang of
ruffians in and around Northampton. For five years he and his
mob terrorised the neighbourhood, until in 1826 he was hanged
for his crimes.

Dick Turpin does not deserve the reputation he has enjoyed
for his daring exploits, like, for instance, his throwing his
pursuers off the scent by reversing his horse's shoes at the Old
Swan in Woughton. He was not always the brave solo-artist,
pitting his wits and skill against authority. For much of his brief
adult life he was a common horse thief, a murderer, and a
member of the Gregory Gang. Though Epping Forest and Essex
were his usual haunts, quite a few of his criminal acts were
done in Bucks., Beds., Northants. and Herts.

Much nearer our own times came the gang from London
who robbed the Mail Train at Bridego Bridge near Linslade and
got away with £2,600,000, and left the engine driver, Jack Mills,
severely injured.

When newspapers and television shock us with details of
some new crime, we might ask ourselves: 'What is the world
coming to?' One answer is that history is merely repeating
itself. If Crimewatch and similar programmes tell us of

Bridego Bridge, Linslade, scene of the Great Train Robbery In 1963. (NK)

robberies, murders, kidnappings and hostage taking, we are right to be shocked. But we would be wrong to assume that these are new phenomena without precedent in the past.

Ever since Cain killed Abel there have been murders – in every age and in every land. Countless individuals have killed other individuals; and countless other individuals have been killed by gangs.

Motives for murder have included greed, envy, rage, jealousy, lust, pride, and every other emotion known to man. Even 'worthy' motives like loyalty have led to murder. The four knights who murdered Thomas à Becket in front of his own altar in Canterbury Cathedral in 1170 did so, not out of hatred for the Archbishop, but out of misplaced loyalty to their king whom they had heard to say: 'Who will rid me of this troublesome priest?'

When today's paper carries the story of the latest outrage it is as well to remember that this is 'not for the first time'. Newspaper files of long ago reveal their precedents.

In 1825 Bishop Stortford in Hertfordshire suffered at the hands of a gang. Their exploits exhibited several of the frightening features which have been repeated many times since then, and still occur today. On April 26 1825 *The Times* carried this report:

INCENDIARIES AT BISHOP'S STORTFORD

'The greatest alarm has prevailed at Bishop's Stortford for several weeks past, in consequence of the diabolical conduct of a set of villains, who, from motives of revenge for the capture and punishment of some of their friends who had been detected in committing several robberies in the neighbourhood, have made several attempts to set the town on fire; and, in one or two of these attempts, they have been so far successful as to do great mischief to several houses. On the night of April 5, a barn, used as a carpenter's shop, belonging to Mr Warner, was set on fire, and that and an adjoining barn, the property of Mr Francis Cole, were completely destroyed. One or two other fires took place, and the inhabitants being placed in a dreadful state of alarm and anxiety, a Committee of respectable persons was formed for the purposes of investigation, and, if possible, prevention of further outrages.*

This Committee held their meetings at the Vestry Room, and at their second or third meeting an anonymous letter was received, addressed: "To the Committee at the Vestry", avowing that the fires that had taken place were the result of a premeditated plan, and threatening that the whole town of Bishop's Stortford should be reduced to ashes unless two persons, named in the letter, were released from prison, and unless the Committee desisted from their endeavours at detection, and withdrew the offers of reward which they had issued.

The Committee still pursued their inquiries, and

early in the morning of the 17th instant the house of Mr William Francis, in North Street, was broken into, and set on fire in two places. At the same time a barn and outhouse were entered and burnt down. Mr Francis, it appears, had taken an active part in the exertions of the Committee. Under these circumstances, application was made to Mr Peel, the Home Secretary, who immediately caused a proclamation to be issued, offering a reward of five hundred guineas for the detection of the offenders, and pardon to any accomplice who should give evidence against his fellows.

An order was given for two active officers of Bow-street to go down and use their utmost exertions to bring the offenders to justice. Bishop and J. J. Smith were sent down last week, and yesterday information was received that they had succeeded in apprehending three men'.

Any crime today is likely to be 'not for the first time'. As Ecclesiastes puts it in the Bible:

'The thing that hath been, it is that that shall be; and that which is done is that which shall be done, and there is no new thing under the sun.'

Chapter 8

NOT IN OUR BACK YARD !

'The rich man in his castle, the poor man at his gate.'

That description only became valid after the Norman Conquest. Before that there scarcely were any castles. After the Conquest an astonishing number were built, almost all of them of the motte and bailey type. Under the feudal system which developed, the landowner and Lord of the Manor could command a proportion of the time and energy of the peasants on his land. In return, the peasants could look to the Lord of the Manor for protection and could also cultivate some of his land for their own use.

The system worked well enough for nearly three centuries. It was radically altered by the Black Death in 1348 which reduced the population by a third. That meant a crippling labour shortage which in its turn sparked off a rise in wages. Government's attempts to curb that rise provoked resentment which exploded in peasants' revolts.

As the population increased, so too did the numbers of the poor. Their needs were largely met by Guilds and monasteries. But with the abolition of the religious houses at the Reformation, this source of help for 'the deserving poor' disappeared. In its place relief began to be initiated in the 16th century by local Justices of the Peace and town councils. But the effect was patchy and something more systematic was needed.

In 1552 for the first time Parliament began to legislate for the care of the poor. It ordered that all parishes should register their poor and seek to meet their needs from local resources.

This was a step in the right direction but it soon proved inadequate. For one thing, it began to be recognised that not all the poor are 'deserving'! Distinction needed to be made between those who could not help themselves, and those who ought to work for their own support.

By Acts passed in 1597 and 1601, the parish continued to be regarded as the unit to care for the poor, but Justices of the Peace were given power to levy a Poor Rate, and to pay for work provided for the able-bodied poor.

The day was coming when the distinction would be made between 'the deserving poor' who needed to be helped, and 'the sturdy beggar' who should be forced to work. As numbers of the poor increased alarmingly, there was danger that among the poor were 'rogues and vagabonds' who were a threat to public order. By all means the 'impotent poor' should be cared for, but 'sturdy beggars' should be made to fend for themselves. As the Scriptures put it: 'If any should not work, neither should he eat'. (2 Thess. 3v10)

So by the end of the 16th century The Poor Law recognised different categories of poor, ranging from the infirm to the

'Sturdy beggars should be whipped'.

dangerous. And in 1598 it was laid down by Statute that beggars were to be whipped.

At the heart of the problem was the principle that each parish should be responsible for dealing with the poor within its boundaries. But why should a parish have to care for poor people who came from elsewhere? To answer that question, Charles II in 1662 passed an Act of Settlement which laid down that every parish was entitled to expel any man, woman, or child from elsewhere and to send them back to their native parish. In other words, the principle of NIOBY could be invoked: NOT IN OUR BACKYARD. So it became a matter of 'Pass the parcel', or perhaps it would be better expressed 'Return to sender'. Every parish tried to expel paupers who came from elsewhere by sending them back as quickly as possible to the places from which they had come.

Responsibility for doing this was laid on the Constables. They were to convey 'vagrants and cripples' to their places of origin. By 1688 a scale of fees was drawn up. A Constable was paid 3d a day for maintaining a vagrant and a further 3d a mile for escorting him back to his place of origin. If that meant a journey of more than ten miles, the Constable could claim 9d a mile.

Hyde, in his 'History of Stony Stratford', uncovered some sharp practice. He noted that the Constables of Little Brickhill and Stony Stratford, responsible for repatriating vagrants to either place, could make a little extra for themselves. Instead of taking the direct route along the Watling Street, they took the vagrants round by 'Woofton' (Woughton). This meant they could charge an extra 1s 6d! But the Justices soon put a stop to that. In 1695 they ordered that vagrants and cripples must be conveyed by the direct route – the Watling Street – and must not be diverted through 'Woofton'.

But while each parish did its best to get rid of unwanted vagrants from other parishes, it was recognised that sometimes a parish would wish to welcome from elsewhere men who were willing to work. So a scheme evolved by which an able-bodied worker might be allowed to move to another parish and be employed there. He could do so if he was provided with a 'Certificate' from his own parish. That Certificate would state that if for any reason the man lost his job in the new parish, his own native parish would have him back and be responsible for his maintenance. In effect these Certificates acted like Passports. If you had one, you were free to settle and work elsewhere. If you had no such Certificate, or had it withdrawn, you were liable to be deported back to your own village.

Such Certificates were regularly in use from 1664 onwards. For a reputable working man, able and willing to work wherever he could find employment, the scheme worked well. But if he lost his job, or fell on hard times, he and his family could still be transported back to the village of their birth, whether they liked it or not.

Evidence that the Certificate scheme was still working in the 1730s is provided by Browne Willis, the Lord of the Manor of Fenny Stratford. He had built St. Martin's as the parish church of Fenny and it was dedicated by the Bishop of Lincoln in 1730. In his usual autocratic way Browne Willis drew up rules about the seating arrangements in the new church. The rules reflect the unashamed class distinctions of the age. After stipulating that home-owners should have the best seats at the front, the rules then direct that 'men and women of an inferior degree' should sit further back in the church. And behind them, still further back, 'the people of the lowest degree, lodgers in the town, or CERTIFICATE PERSONS' who are to sit right at the back under the gallery.

Meanwhile, what about the poor who belong to the parish, and cannot be shunted off elsewhere? The parish authorities could not invoke the NIOBY principle against their own poor; they had a right to stay in their own village or town.

As early as the 15th century Church Guilds had tried to make some provision for the poor. Work Houses, or Poor Houses, began to be built. They were usually unattractive both in design and regime. Furniture and diet were uniformly uninspiring; accommodation in dormitories segregated the

Quainton Almshouses. Such almshouses were vastly superior to later Poor Houses. (JH)

sexes, so husbands and wives were parted. It is true that almshouses were often built by charitable individuals and these were of a much better quality than the common Work Houses.

Each Poor House or Work House was run by a Master. He was hardly better off than the inmates he supervised. His wage was often a meagre 4s a week, though he had his own accommodation – not at all lavish – and his food. He was answerable to the Overseers who were elected annually. In their turn the Overseers were answerable to the Justices of the Peace who scrutinised the Overseers' accounts.

From 1723 the Work House Test Act obliged the poor to enter Workhouses to obtain relief. But this provision was emended in 1782 by excluding from Workhouses the able-bodied poor. For them the parish was obliged to provide either work or 'outdoor relief'. In 1795 the so-called Speenhamland system was introduced. Under this scheme farm labourers' wages were supplemented from Parish Rates on a scale depending on wheat prices and family size. The system

survived until 1834 when the new Poor Law Amendment Act was passed.
This Act created six hundred unions of parishes, each group having one Union Workhouse. The Newport Pagnell Union was one of the first to be set up under the Act. Parishes within the Newport Union were: Astwood, Bletchley, Bow Brickhill, Bradwell, Bradwell Abbey, Broughton, Castlethorpe, Chicheley, Clifton Reynes, Cold Brayfield, Emberton, Fenny Stratford, Gayhurst, Haversham, Lathbury, Lavendon, Little Brickhill, Little Linford, Little Woolstone, Loughton, Milton Keynes, Moulsoe, Newport Pagnell, Newton Blossomville, Newton Longville, North Crawley, Olney, Olney Park Farm, Petsoe Manor, Ravenstone, Shenley Church End, Sherington, Simpson, Stantonbury, Stoke Goldington, Tyringham-cum-Filgrave, Walton, Warrington, Water Eaton, Wavendon, Weston Underwood, Willen and Woughton-on-the-Green.

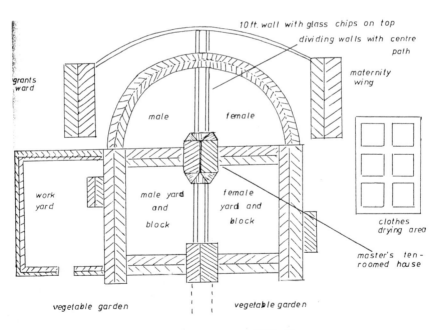

Sketch plan of Newport Pagnell Workhouse.
Newport Pagnell Union, one of the first to be built.

A Board of Governors was needed to run the Union. Its first task was to erect suitable buildings, to accommodate some 3–400 persons. It was done in stages. The first house for fifty paupers was opened on February 25th 1837. Other buildings were later added.

Later generations came to know the institution as Rennie Lodge. With the passage of time it ceased altogether to be the 'Workhouse' and became a geriatric hospital under the NHS. It was finally closed in 1991 and has now been demolished.

The True Tale of Widow Tucker

This brief account has touched on some of the ways in which society over the centuries has tried to deal with the poor. Perhaps the case of one individual is needed to give the subject human scale. That one individual could well be Widow Tucker.

She had been born in Stony Stratford but moved to Northampton when she married. Three sons were born to the marriage but then the husband died. His widow was left with three young children to bring up, the eldest being thirteen. Widow Tucker grew ill and was a virtual cripple. She got behind with her rent.

On March 4th 1830, 'in pain and distress, and racket with pains in my limes', she wrote this letter to the Overseers of the Poor in Stony Stratford:

'The Lord thought wel to lay upon my family the smorlpoxes, likewise the loss of looving husbaman . . . I have under the neseity of sending to you respekting of my rent. A half yeares is dew wich is £3 and if it is not paid I shall have my goods sould from me and my Bed from under me thath I lie upon. I hope Gentlemen that you will take it in consadrashion and alow that I may stop at Northampton with my famley. I humble if you will pay the rent for me this time may it be the last, for my harte is overwhelmed with trouble . . . So now no more from me at this time.

M. Tucker, Tanne Street, Northampton.'

It seemed to the Overseers in Stony Stratford that there were two alternatives – either send her money to help with her rent, or bring her back to her native Stony Stratford and accommodate her and her family in the Stony Stratford Poor House. They decided on the latter course. They wrote to the widow's landlord in Northampton asking for a list of the widow's effects. Their intention was to sell her goods and bring the family back to Stratford.

The landlord, Mr Simpson, replied:

*'According to your wish I send you the following
list of Widow Tuckley's furniture:*

Then follows a pathetic list of the widow's few goods. Incidentally, in the correspondence the widow sometimes appears as Tucker and sometimes as Tuckley. Mr Simpson's letter concludes:

*'She seems very desirous to stop here, and if you will
allow her 1s a week to her rent extra she will by some
means make up the rent. Her son, a steady lad, is an
apprentice, and hopes to be a comfort to her and to assist
her in a little time; the next boy is at the foundry, twelve
years of age; she can wash for and lodge him. She expects
they will take him as an apprentice.'*

Despite this, the Stratford Overseers decided they would sell up the widow and bring her and her family back to Stratford. But the landlord tried again. He wrote:

*'I have seen the widow Tuckley, and it does not appear
she can pay one shilling of the back rent £3 1s 0d. I am
not willing to take to her goods, unless you make up your
minds not to discharge it, and the few of her goods that
she might do without it would take to pay the rent of the
present month. Were I to go for the remainder of my
claim she would not have a bed to lay on or a chair to sit*

on. You will excuse me, Sir, but I think that if you pay the £3 1s 0d the poor woman may manage to get through. It would grieve me, and I think you too, after the afflictions of her family, and the love of her husband, to have everything they have worked for to be took away for rent'.

This time the Stratford Overseers accepted the landlord's advice. They voted relief for the widow at 6s 6d a week. But a little later they wondered if they had been too generous. They decided to consult their opposite number, the Northampton Overseers, who replied:

'I have seen Widow Tucker and enquired particularly as to her situation. There are three children of the age 13, 9, and 4. The eldest does a little towards maintenance. The woman is very lame and in bad health, and cannot earn anything toward supporting the family and I really think the present allowance not too much for their absolute necessities.'

So Widow Tucker was allowed to end her days in Northampton after all. Her story shows that Authority could be sensitive to the plight of an individual.

But not every time. The Tucker correspondence is dated 1830. In that very same year the Justices of the Peace meeting in Aylesbury sent a letter to all Church Wardens and Overseers. It said:

'Workhouses should be established for the able poor willing to work. The pauper who should refuse or run away from such work to be liable to hard labour on conviction of any JP in the neighbourhood for a period of one to three months.'

The Circular went on to urge the leasing of land 'in order to give additional facility for the employment of infant labour, and generally to decrease the burthen of the poor rates.' And finally the Circular resolved 'to disallow and strike out all items which shall appear in Overseers's accounts not in accordance with the spirit of the forthgoing resolutions'.

The NIOBY principle – 'Not in Our Back Yard' – continued to permit forcible repatriation of paupers until 1865. In that year the Union Chargeability Act abolished the old rule. 'Settlement Certificates' were also abolished. Labour was at last free to go where it wished in search of work. But the Unions or Workhouses remained, grim reminders of the unhappy plight of the poor. Only in the 20th century would they disappear.

Chapter 9

WHATEVER HAPPENED TO— ?

One Shilling and Sixpence

On 11 November 1724 Browne Willis laid the Foundation Stone of the new St. Martin's Church that he was building in Fenny Stratford. The Lord of the Manor later said that the building of that church , (the first Parish Church Fenny had ever had), was his 'chiefest and most real worldly comfort and happiness'.

He built the church on the site of an ancient Chantry Chapel which had been pulled down after the Reformation. That had

St. Martin;s Church, Fenny Stratford. On the left, the church as built in 1730. On the right, the 19h century extension.

happened just before Elizabeth I came to the throne. Being the historian he was, Browne Willis marked that foundation-stone-laying ceremony by placing under the Stone an Elizabethan silver shilling. His son was also present that day and had his part to play in the ceremony. Under his stone he placed an Elizabethan silver sixpence.

All very symbolic. And we can be sure that those present that day had the historic significance of it all pointed out to them by Browne Willis.

But there is a mystery. Search for those Foundation Stones today and you will not find them. There is absolutely no sign of them. So whatever happened to those one shilling and sixpenny Elizabethan silver coins?

The Canon and the Coins

Charles I raised his standard at Nottingham on 15 August 1642 and thus marked the beginning of the Civil War, One of the

On this hill Charles I raised his Standard in Nottingham in 1642. The Civil War followed. (JH)

earliest adherents to rally to his cause was Sir Richard Minshull of Bourton in Buckinghamshire. The Parliamentarians determined to make an example of Sir Richard. They sent a force on 18 August 1642 under Lord Brooke to attack his house with cannons and left it in ruins.

A relic from that incident, a cannon used in the attack, was dug up in 1839 near Thornborough Bridge on the Bletchley to Buckingham road. The Duke of Buckingham presented the historic cannon to Buckingham Borough Council who erected it in the town so as to prevent traffic from mounting the pavement. The original bore of the cannon was filled with cement. But before this was done Alderman Harrison inserted into the barrel of the cannon a bottle containing coins and other items.

Some years later the old cannon was knocked over and removed. But no trace of its contents were found.

Cromwell's Body

On 14 June 1645 the Battle of Naseby virtually brought the Civil War to an end. Cromwell and the Roundheads had won. And Cromwell himself had played a significant part in that battle. The dashing Prince Rupert had made one of his celebrated cavalry charges which might have carried the day for the Royalists. But Cromwell on the right flank of the battlefield had bided his time and then wheeled round and led his Roundhead cavalry into the rear of the Royalist centre.

Cromwell went on to become the Lord Protector; King Charles was executed; and for eleven years England became a Republic.

Cromwell died on 3 September 1658. What happened then? Well, the answer comes in two different versions. The official version, in the history books, is that Cromwell's body lay in state in Westminster Abbey. But then the monarchy was restored in 1660 and Charles II came to the throne amid general rejoicing. Cromwell's body was then dug up, his head was detached and stuck on a pike at Westminster. His body was hanged at Tyburn and afterwards buried there. A sad episode in our nation's history.

Death Warrant of Charles I. Nine of the regicides who signed it were from Buckinghamshire.

But there is the second version to consider. This says that when the crowds flocked to Westminster Hall for the lying-in-state, what they actually saw was only a waxen effigy. His real body, this version claims, was carried off secretly to Naseby in Northamptonshire, to the very scene of that crucial battle of thirteen years before. And there, secretly, it was buried in a grave nine feet deep. The turf was then carefully relaid over the grave. Later, the field was ploughed and planted with corn. So no trace ever remained of that burial of Oliver Cromwell.

So what did happen to Cromwell's body? You have a choice between two answers!

❖ ❖ ❖ ❖ ❖

Boudica's Body

Sixteen centuries before anybody might ask what happened to Cromwell's body, the same question could be asked about Boudica's body. And in this case too Northamptonshire figures in the story.

The redoubtable Boudica was Queen of the Iceni tribe and she proved more than a handful for the Romans to cope with. In 61AD the Roman army was preoccupied with putting down unrest in North Wales. Boudica chose that time to go on the rampage. Her army seized and sacked Camulodunum (Colchester) and then set fire to Londinium (London). They then advanced on Verulamium (St. Albans) and reduced it to ashes. In these battles some 70,000 Romans and Roman sympathisers were killed.

The Romans rallied. Their troops returned from the North Wales campaign and other Roman units marched down from Lincolnshire. All was now set for the great showdown – between Boudica and her Iceni army, and the Roman Ninth Legion. An horrific battle ensued and this time Boudica was comprehensively defeated. Thousands of her tribesmen were killed.

Where did that great battle take place? The answer almost

certainly is that it was in the forest areas of South Northants. Boudica was not killed in that battle but she took her own life, by poison.

So we come to the question – Whatever happened to Boudica's body? Once more there seem to be alternative answers. One answer says that Queen Boudica was buried in the area which centuries later would become the part of London where the great Railway Stations of Kings Cross and St. Pancras would arise.

The alternative theory is quite different. It says that Boudica was buried (together with a great quantity of golden regalia) in the very general area where her last battle was fought, namely in Whittlewood Forest.

Is there any evidence to support such a theory? Well, in the reign of Edward I (1272–1307) a deed was granted relating to land in Wittlebury. The deed describes the land as being near 'Dedequenemor'. A similar deed in the same period describes other land as being adjacent to 'le dedequene fourlong'.

Who was the dead queen referred to in 'Dedequenemor' (Dead Queen's Moor)? And in 'dedequene fourlong' (Dead Queen Furlong)? It might very well be that here we have the answer to the question: Whatever happened to Boudica's body?

The Cub Reporter from the Morning Chronicle
Whatever happened to him? In the ordinary course of events his future might not excite anyone's interest. But his case is different.

He was only a young junior on the staff of *The Morning Chronicle*. 'Go down,' they said, 'to Kettering and report on the election there.' So the Cub reporter came to Kettering and filed his story in 1835. He was only twenty-three years old.

How good a story he sent to *The Morning Chronicle* doesn't matter much. On that visit he met the Watson family of Rockingham Castle. He met them again later and they became great friends.

*Rockingham Castle. Dickens wrote
part of David Copperfield here.*

That Cub Reporter went on to become one of the greatest
English authors of all time. His name was Charles Dickens. He
stayed often as a guest at rockingham Castle, and wrote much
of David Copperfield there. He knew Towcester well too, and it
became the locale for parts of Pickwick Papers.

❖ ❖ ❖ ❖ ❖

The Pitstone Hill White Horse
The White Horse was the Standard of the ancient Saxons. So it is
not surprising that in various places in England the White Horse
has been 'carved' on hillsides. In truth it is very easily done. On
chalk hills, if you remove the turf, you expose the white chalk.

They did this at Uffington in Berkshire, and the White
Horse there commemorates Alfred's great victory over the
Danes in 871. But there are several others elsewhere, notably
the White Horse at Westbury in Wiltshire.

But a White Horse on Pitstone Hill? There is no sign of one.
Yet it seems highly likely that there was once a White Horse
there. Intrinsically it would be a very apt place for such a
monument. Across the hill ran the ancient Icknield Way, and
also Grimm's Ditch. Archaeological excavations have yielded
traces of Iron Age Settlements, a Saxon Cemetery, and Roman
settlements. Clearly Pitstone Hill has been of great importance
over the early centuries.

In 1530 Henry Partridge of Aldbury died. In his will he bequeathed an area of ground in North Field 'adjacent to a way called White Horse Waye'. Fifty years before that, in 1580, a sale was agreed to between Thomas Turnour of Hemel Hempstead, and Francis Wynche of Aldbury. The land being sold included 'three roods in Nokeden Furlong butting into Whight Horse'. Nokeden, or Noke Deane, was also in North Field.

It does look probable, then, that before 1580 a White Horse had been cut into the chalk on Pitstone Hill. Whatever happened to it? Much quarrying by Tunnel Cement may have cut away the hill where the White Horse once was. Or it may be that the higher parts of the hill, not affected by quarrying, may still be hiding the White Horse which once existed.

❖ ❖ ❖ ❖ ❖

The Coffins and the Manuscripts

Shakespeare's grand-daughter, Lady Elizabeth Barnard, died at Abington Manor in 1669, aged sixty-four. It was said that she had inherited many precious Shakespeare manuscripts. If so, whatever happened to them? The rumour that they were concealed somewhere in Abington Manor is discounted by the fact that in about 1740 new owners of the house had it largely rebuilt. The manuscripts would surely have come to light then, if indeed they were hidden in the house.

Were they, perhaps, not hidden in the house, but in Lady Elizabeth's tomb? She died in 1669 and her burial is recorded under that date in the Abington Parish Register. Her husband

William Shakespeare. Are some of his hidden manuscripts waiting to be discovered in Northampton?

had died before and had been buried in the church. His widow would certainly have been laid to rest in her late husband's tomb.

But the coffins of both have disappeared. Were they, at some time removed from the tomb in church and then re-interred in the churchyard? If so, where?

Other questions come to mind.

Were the alleged missing Shakespeare manuscripts buried with Lady Elizabeth in her coffin? Were they, perhaps stolen from her coffin in 1807, when thieves broke into the church and stole its silverware?

Or did Lady Elizabeth deliberately hide the manuscripts, and take the secret of their whereabouts with her to the grave? She had lived through the Puritan years under Oliver Cromwell, a time when all theatres were closed, and all theatrical connections were scorned and legislated against.

Whatever answers are made to these questions, the mysteries remain. Whatever happened to those coffins, and will those precious manuscripts one day be discovered to excite us all?

Chapter 10

SENSATION AND SCANDAL !

They called him 'Old Wrinkle Boots' because his dress was as eccentric as his manner. He was Browne Willis, Lord of the three Manors of Whaddon, Bletchley and Fenny Stratford. He was an antiquarian, historian and church benefactor, and he gave Fenny Stratford its first parish church, St. Martin's, in 1730.

He was an author too. Several of his books gave details about all the Cathedrals of England and Wales. They do not make easy reading. In fact one reviewer said of them: 'It is as if he has written the index and forgotten to write the book'.

But that criticism could not be levelled at another of his books. This was: 'History and Antiquities of the Town, Hundred and Deanry of Buckingham'. In it he covers first the history of the town from Domesday up to the 18th century. He then moves out into the countryside and proceeds 'to treat the Hamlets appendent to it'. In nearly four hundred pages he lavishes his meticulous and erudite scholarship on all the villages around Buckingham. The amount of detail is almost overwhelming.

While all of it is fascinating to any reader with a sense of history, one chapter stands out as being positively sensational! That chapter deals with the quite astounding goings-on in the little village of Water Stratford in the 1690s.

Browne Willis begins the chapter calmly enough, with no hint of the revelations to come. He tells us first about Water Stratford's origins – its entry in the Domesday Survey, the families who held the Manor in successive reigns, the

THE

HISTORY and ANTIQUITIES

OF THE

Town, Hundred, and Deanry

OF

BUCKINGHAM:

CONTAINING, A

DESCRIPTION

OF THE

TOWNS,	MONASTERIES,	CHANTRIES,
VILLAGES,	CHURCHES,	SEATS,
HAMLETS,	CHAPELS,	MANORS,

Their ANTIENT and PRESENT OWNERS;

TOGETHER WITH THE

EPITAPHS, INSCRIPTIONS, and ARMS

In all the PARISH CHURCHES;

AND

STATE of the RECTORIES, VICARAGES, DONATIVES; their PATRONS, and INCUMBENTS, TERRIERS, and VALUATIONS in the KING's BOOKS.

Also some Account of the

EARLS and DUKES of BUCKINGHAM,

AND

HIGH-SHERIFFS of the COUNTY.

With a Tranſcript out of Domeſday-Book, and the Tranſlation thereof into Engliſh.

COLLECTED from Records, Leiger-Books, antient Manuſcripts, Evidences, Regiſters, and other ſelect Authorities.

By BROWNE WILLIS, Eſq; LL.D.

LONDON:

Printed for the AUTHOR, M,DCC,LV.

Browne Willis published his History of Buckingham in 1755.

geographical location, and the connections with Luffield Priory. And then, when the reader has been lulled into quiet interest in all this history, he suddenly detonates his bombshell! Read it now as Browne Willis relates it:

'In the years 1693 and 1694, this Place was much resorted unto on account its Rector, Mr John Mason, who taught publicly that he had seen Christ, and that He had at this Place begun His personal Reign on Earth; which enthusiastical Predictions occasioned great Resort hither from many Parts of the Neighbourhood, insomuch that all the Barns and Houses hereabouts were filled with his Followers, many of whom were so infatuated that they sold their Estates, being persuaded that this World was at an end; and so took up their Abodes and dwelt here some Years after his death.

He having given it out that he should rise again in Three days, his adherents were so possessed with the Belief thereof, that his Successor in the Rectory, Mr

Water Stratford Church, scene of astonishing events in 1693. (JH)

Rushworth informed me that he was obliged to open his Grave, expose his Corpse, and thereby convince the People of the Madness of his Tenets.

There were, as I have seen, some Pamphlets wrote to explode his Doctrine, particularly one by the Reverend Mr Henry Maurice, Rector of Tyringham, which is entitled 'An impartial Account of Mr John Mason of Water Stratford and his sentiments.'

At this point Browne Willis interrupts his own narrative to bring in testimony from another source. He writes:

'But as I have (while I am printing this history) been favoured with a more particular Account thereof, I shall here insert it as it was transmitted to me, in a letter from a Gentleman and Lady, seated at the next Parish. Their Account of Mr Mason is as follows:

"Mr Mason being a popular Preacher, the common People, especially the Women, came from far and near to be his Auditors; and as he came out of the Church, the People used to kneel down and beg his Blessing, and he laid his Hands on them and blessed them, as our Bishops now do. It is thought this was the first occasion of his spiritual Pride, which afterwards led him into Extasies and pretended Revelations.

He told his congregation, (which was composed of whole families, some of whom sold their Estates and Lands, and brought their Substance to Water Stratford, where they brew'd, bak'd, roast'd and boyl'd in a Notable Manner), that our Lord Christ would appear at Water Stratford, and come and judge the world on Whitsunday following.

They went out most Evenings into the Fields and sung their Hymns; My grandfather and Mother went out to see them. The first object they met with was a Countryman, who lay on his face in Water Stratford

Churchyard, who was quite tired with singing; and when turned on his Back was speechless but came to himself. Then they went into the Parsonage House, and there was a Congregation walking round the Hall in a Ring, making a prodigious Noise, and all of them crying out GLORY, GLORY, GLORY, and all in a Sweat and looking as if they were mad. My Mother told them she thought their's was an odd Way of serving God, and wish'd they were not mad. At which they all stood still with their Mouths open, and stared fiercely on her, but said nothing, and she verily believes if my Grandfather and another Gentleman had not been with her with their swords by their sides, they would have served her as they did Mrs Lisle of Imly, whose Head-Cloaths they pulled-off, and cried: AVOID SATAN! Then my Mother said: 'Poor deluded people, I am sorry for you. I wish I could speak with Mr Mason'. Then one of their Women went upstairs, and brought down Word that Mr Mason was not to be seen or spoke with.

Some time after came the Duke of Richmond and a great many more noble Persons, who tho' denied access to him, forced their Way up to him, and talked to him a good deal. And amongst other Things he told them he had seen our Lord Christ in the Room where they were then, with his fleshly eyes and spoke to him with his fleshly Tongue; and that our Lord Christ told him that he would come and appear in the Air over Water Stratford, and judge the World on Whitsunday following.

After this he looked out of his Chamber Window and said the same things to the Multitude that stood underneath. After this he was struck speechless, which was occasioned (as is supposed) by over talking himself; on which Dr Paxton, (a very eminent Physician), was sent for from Buckingham, who came from visiting Mr Mason to our House, and told my

Father and Mother that Mr Mason's Ail was a Squinancy, and that he would not recover, and he accordingly died of it. He told his Auditory when he was alive that he should rise the third Day after his disease, and with his Body ascend into Heaven.

He was buried before the third Day, and several of his People averring that they had seen him and spoke to him after his Resurrection on a Piece of Ground or Close behind the Parsonage House, which they called Holy Ground; his successor, the Reverend Mr Rushworth, thought proper to take his Body up, and had the Coffin opened, and showed them the Corps.

But this did not satisfy them; still they would meet on Holy Ground, as they called it, and did so for sundry years; and when Mr Rushworth discharged them from coming there, they assembled in an House in Water Stratford.

In the year 1710 (fifteen years after his death) on a Sunday, my Mother and a neighbouring Lady went and saw them there, and they sung the same Hymns and made the same Noise, and went round in a Ring as they used to do.

There are none of them that now assemble on this Holy Ground, as the Sect seems to be quite extinct for these last twelve years. I need not tell you that our Lord Christ did not appear as Mr Mason said He would. I think the chief Thing this new Sect or Religion produced was that several women had their Bellies raised, it being one of their fundamental Articles to have all Things common amongst them"'

Browne Willis makes no comment himself on this delicate implication that there was a sexual dimension to these extraordinary events. Instead he goes on to inform his readers about current publications printed in London to tell the world what had been going on in remotest Buckinghamshire!

So that is Browne Willis's account of the astonishing career of the Rector of Water Stratford. But what Browne Willis does not explain is the tortured background to John Mason's eccentricity. The fact is that long before Mason became obsessed with the imminent ENDING of the world ('next Whitsunday!'), he had previously suffered from an opposite obsession – about the BEGINNING of the world. That obsession took the form of an intense study of biblical chronology. Mason thought it was possible, by assigning dates to every person and incident recorded in the Old Testament, to arrive at the precise date when Creation occurred.

He spent weeks and months on this study and finally published his conclusions. And they were dismissed out of hand – nobody wanted to know. This left Mason shattered. At this low ebb in his life, his wife died. Perhaps the double tragedy unhinged his mind, and from then on a religious mania possessed him.

Browne Willis described Mason's behaviour as 'enthusiastical seduction'. That might sound an understatement, till one realises that to an 18th century writer like Browne Willis 'enthusiasm' meant 'fanatical religious ardour'. From its Greek derivation, the word 'enthusiasm' implies 'ecstasy from supposed possession by a god'. And that, in its turn, reminds one of the old saying: 'Whom the gods love, they first make mad'.

Chapter 11

PERSONALITY PARADE

One of the dictionary definitions of personality is: 'A person of prominence or notoriety, a celebrity, a character'.

Earl Cardigan of Deene in Northamptonshire surely qualifies. He used his immense wealth to make his regiment, the 11th Hussars, the smartest in the British Army. But he also gave the fatal order for his cavalry to charge the Russian guns at Balaclava on 25th October 1854 in the Crimean War. Only 194 men our of 670 survived that suicidal attack. 'The Charge of the Light Brigade', though it totally failed of its purpose, nevertheless made Cardigan a popular hero in Britain.

Far more of a personality was his second wife. She was Miss de Horsey until she became the second Lady Cardigan. She survived her husband's death for nearly half a century, and she was a true eccentric.

She commissioned a marble effigy of Lord Cardigan for his tomb in Deene Church. She also commissioned a beautiful statue of herself which was placed beside that of her husband. So for well over forty years before she herself died, her statue graced the tomb in Deene Church.

Nor was that all. She had her own coffin made many years before she died. She kept it on trestles in the ballroom of her house. Sometimes she would invite guests to lie in it and to report on its comfort.

She worshipped regularly in the parish church, occupying the family pew, always accompanied by her two dogs who were famous for their reverent behaviour. In fact their behaviour was better than that of their mistress, who frequently said in a loud voice: 'What utter rot' if she didn't like what the preacher was saying.

❖

Much lower down the social scale was Mrs Wootton. Her husband was a notorious poacher. For thirty years he poached deer in the forests of South Northants. Time after time warrants were issued for his arrest. One night, when he had no less than three deer carcasses in his house, the authorities came yet again to arrest him. He had been warned of their coming, but there was too little time for him to do much about it.

But Mrs Wootton was equal to the occasion. She quickly undressed and donned her nightgown. Then she jumped into bed with the three carcasses hidden under her blankets. The rangers came and stormed into the house to search it. When they came to the bedroom the cool Mrs Wootton patted the lumps under the blankets and said: 'Lie still, my dears, the naughty men won't hurt you'.

❖

Paul Pindar was born in the Poor House in Wellingborough in the 16th century. Despite his deprived beginning he got enough education to become himself a teacher at the local Grammar School. He might well have gone to University but he had other ambitions.

In about 1580 he went up to London and was apprenticed to an Italian merchant there. Though he was only twenty his Italian master thought sufficiently highly of him to send him as his Agent to the Levant. Within fifteen years Pindar had earned through commissions a huge personal fortune for himself. He built himself a magnificent house in London.

In 1603 James I succeeded Elizabeth I. He needed to find a new Ambassador to serve at Constantinople, and he chose Paul Pindar. Paul became as efficient and successful in this new role as in everything else to which he set his hand. English trade with Turkey benefited enormously and his own personal fortune grew too. He was knighted for his services and by the time he returned to England he was worth a least a quarter of a million.

He brought with him from Turkey a magnificent diamond, valued at £35,000. King James himself admired the great stone and wanted to buy it. But Sir Paul Pindar refused to sell it. However, on state occasions, he lent the great diamond to the King.

King James died in 1625 and was succeeded by his son, Charles I. King Charles knew all about the diamond and he too wished to own it. This time Sir Paul Pindar agreed to sell, so the King bought the gem for £18,000. But he never ever paid for it – he was always strapped for cash. And Sir Paul Pindar was too devoted a royalist to press for payment. In the end the ill-fated King Charles pawned the Pindar diamond in Holland.

Sir Paul Pindar lived to be eighty-five, dying in 1650. Long after his death his magnificent house at Bishopsgate, where he had so often entertained both King James and King Charles, became an Inn in 1787 and was known as 'The Paul Pindar'. The building was finally pulled down when Liverpool Street Station was enlarged.

There are still some reminders of the beneficence of the man who had been born in the Poor House in Wellingborough. Peterborough Cathedral has some silver altar plate donated by him. So also does Wellingborough Parish Church.

❖

Wellingborough also provides the story of another personality – a sad story this time. In the Civil War Wellingborough sided with the King, while Northampton's sympathies were with the Roundheads.

The Vicar of Wellingborough, named Jones, was seventy years old. Roughnecks from Northampton raided Wellingborough and carried off their booty to Northampton. They returned a second time to do the same thing again. This time they seized the old Vicar and determined to have some sport with him. They had earlier murdered a barber and stolen his bear. The bear, used in the barbarous sport of bear-baiting, was a savage creature of very uncertain temperament.

The roughs from Northampton thought what fun it would be to mount the septuagenarian Vicar of Wellingborough on the bear's back. They did so, and assumed he would be savaged and killed at once. But as soon as the bear was released by its handlers, with the Vicar on its back, it became utterly docile, and carried the old man along. This angered and disappointed the mob. One of them threw the old man off the bear and mounted it himself. At once the bear turned vicious. It threw off its tormentor and savaged him to death.

That would be a suitable point at which to conclude this recital. But, sadly, there is more to tell. The old Vicar was thrown into prison in Northampton and died there. To his shame, the Mayor of Northampton, John Giffard, ordered that the only burial service the Vicar should be given was that he should be put into a grave, with only the Words:

'Ashes to ashes, dust to dust,
Here's the pit and in you must'.

❖

Fate was much kinder to another parson. His name was John Moore and he was the impecunious Curate of Brackley. A rich business man in the town was John Watts. He befriended the young curate and often entertained him at his house. On one occasion he lent the poor Curate £10. When the Curate was unable to repay the loan he felt too ashamed to continue to enjoy the business man's hospitality, so he went no more to the rich man's house for dinner. The rich man learned why the Curate stayed away and persuaded him to resume his visits for dinner.

Later, the Curate was appointed to a good living. From then on his progress was steadily upwards. Eventually he became the Most Reverend John Moore, Archbishop of Canterbury!

Meanwhile the business man's affairs in Brackley were moving in the opposite direction. The Plumbing business, which had been the foundation of his success, suddenly failed. He and his wife found themselves almost paupers.

Archbishop Moore learned of this and promptly sent money to help his old friend. From then on he paid Mr and Mrs Watts an Annuity. When Watts died, the Archbishop continued the Annuity to his widow.

Then Archbishop Moore died. But the Archbishop's widow then continued paying the Annuity. And when the Archbishop's widow died, her son continued to pay the Annuity. And this went on until, in 1821, Mrs Watts herself died, aged ninety-six.

❖

Here to end this Personality Parade is the true tale not of one Personality, but of a trio of them. They were all peers of the realm, all members of the House of Lords, and all neighbours to each other in Northamptonshire. They found themselves in fierce competition with each other.

The occasion was an election in Northampton in 1768. There were three candidates competing for the two seats available. Their Lordships backed rival candidates. They followed the customs of the age in using bribery and corruption to support the candidates of their choice.

Lord Halifax invited the voters to Horton Hall and plied them with prodigious quantities of wine from his cellars. Without giving any assurance that they would support the candidate of Lord Halifax's choice, the voters then went on to Castle Ashby and drank deeply there at Lord Northampton's expense. And, finally, the voters staggered on to Althorp and refreshed themselves still further at Lord Spencer's expense.

But Lord Spencer gave the episode a new dimension. Powdered footmen stood at the main door of Althorp and presented sandwiches to all the voters. And in each sandwich there was concealed a golden guinea.

But even this artistic touch didn't do the trick. Lord Spencer's candidate failed to get a seat. Nothing daunted, Lord Spencer appealed against the result of the election. The hearing of the Appeal to the House of Commons lasted six weeks and was staggeringly expensive.

Lord Spencer won the Appeal, so his candidate got one of the two seats. Lords Northampton and Halifax then tossed up to see which candidate should have the second seat. But the whole fiasco brought ruin to them both. Lord Halifax had to sell Horton Hall, and Lord Northampton, although he didn't have to sell Castle Ashby, he couldn't afford to live in it either. He shut the house up and lived the rest of his life in voluntary exile abroad.

Chapter 12

HOW PECULIAR !

You would expect there to be a distinction between the ordinary and the peculiar. That which is ordinary is of established or common type or occurrence; it is familiar, everyday, commonplace; it is unexceptional, even uninteresting.

On the other hand, that which is peculiar is strange or unusual; it is distinct from others and has some special characteristic; it borders on the exotic.

Both words however have other meanings as well. These bring them into a fascinating relationship set in the context of church authority and ecclesiastical history.

Thus the word 'ordinary' in the Church of England means the ecclesiastic who has jurisdiction – in other words the Bishop of the Diocese. Or, at a higher level still, the Archbishop of the Province. They are 'ordinary' because they exercise regular oversight in their own right. They keep order, and the very word 'ordinary' comes from the Latin word 'ordo', meaning exactly that, 'order'.

The word 'peculiar' in the Church of England can mean a parish or group of parishes exempt from the jurisdiction of the Ordinary of the Diocese. In medieval times there were a great number of these. Mostly they were monastic peculiars, coming under the rule and authority of the Abbot of a religious order rather than the Diocesan bishop. Others were 'royal peculiars'.

Early in the 19th century there were still over three hundred peculiars. Between 1838 and 1850 nearly all of these were abolished. But not all. Some peculiars survive to this day. These include cathedral peculiars related to Westminster Abbey, and royal peculiars related to royal residences, such as St. George's Chapel, Windsor, and the Chapel Royal of the Savoy in London. Other surviving examples are the peculiars of Battle, Bocking, Jersey and Guernsey.

Let the Record Show
The ancient parish of St. Mary Magdalene, Little Brickhill, was a peculiar of the Archbishop of Canterbury. As such it was exempt from the jurisdiction of the Ordinary, i.e. at that time the Bishop of Lincoln.

Little Brickhill Church – a 'Peculiar'. (JH)

One effect of this was that the incumbent of Little Brickhill was empowered to issue licences for marriage without having to seek the permission or authority of the diocese.

This made the parish a popular place of resort for marriages. Marriage could be sought there with less publicity than the parties concerned would encounter in their own parishes.

In an age when non-conformity was made very difficult, by seeking to be married at Little Brickhill non-conformists could escape the embarrassment of having to go to their local parish church to be married.

Geography played a part too. Little Brickhill lies right on the Watling Street. It was a place, therefore, well accustomed to the comings and goings of strangers and travellers. Any such strangers, intent on matrimony, could be well served by the Vicar of the peculiar parish of Little Brickhill, able to issue them with a licence to marry.

It was a useful fact, too, that Little Brickhill being right on the Watling Street made a convenient meeting place for couples whose families lay at a distance on either side of the village.

Between 1559 and 1752 the Parish Registers show that well over one thousand one hundred marriages were solemnised in the parish – a large number for so small a village. Of course many of those marriages were of couples either or both of whom were resident in the parish. But quite a number, too, were solemnised for couples neither of whom were local residents.

But in 1653 the Puritans, under Cromwell, enacted that henceforth marriage should no longer be solemnised by a priest, but by the Justice of the Peace. And the same law required that couples should notify their intention to wed on three Sundays before they presented themselves to the JP to have their marriage ratified.

This attack on the pastoral duties of the parish priest was meant to apply to every parish. It was fiercely resented by many. No doubt it often happened that even though couples were married by the JP. they and their parish priest would contrive that their marriages should also be blessed sacramentally and privately.

What was the effect of the new law on the rights of the incumbent of the peculiar parish of Little Brickhill? Well, a note appears in the Register of 1653 saying:

'Seene and approved according to the late Act of Parliament for Maryages, births and buryalls according

to the Certificate of the Parishioners Anno Dom 1653 November 14'.

Thereafter, until at the Restoration of Charles II in 1660 that Puritan law was rescinded, Little Brickhill Registers record fourteen marriages under the Act. The wording used in the Register in each case is:

'Intention of Maryage between .... and .... was published in the said Parish Church three several Lords Days at the close of the morning exercise and the said persons .... and .... were maryed before .... JP on (date)'.

The same Act had decreed that births of children should be recorded, not baptisms. In the years from 1653 up to the Restoration Registers in Little Brickhill seem to have been kept in duplicate for the purposes of recording baptisms. One set records baptisms in the ordinary way, while the other set records births rather than baptisms of infants. The device used seems to have been that for the years 1658–9 the birth dates were recorded among the burials.

Because of its location on the Watling Street the village of Little Brickhill was from time to time the venue for the Assize Courts. Many of the cases heard there resulted in sentences of death. This is grimly reflected in the Little Brickhill Registers. Thus:

1562 July 9
SMITH, William, DICKSON, William, RENSTLER, Peter, DAY, William, SHAKESPEARE, James, suffered death and were buryed

1595 Mar 26
BUTTERFIELD, Robert, DOULEY, Steven, SMITH, William, LEWEN, William, RIE, John, BENCHAM, Richard, VAUGHAN, John, BURROWES, Dorell, BUCKMINSTER, Edmund, PHILLIPES, Robert, suffered death and were buryed.

Similar entries appear also in 1570,1583, 1587, 1588, 1617 and 1618. Altogether, between 1563 and 1618 forty-six executed prisoners were buried at Little Brickhill.

Other burial entries in the Little Brickhill Registers are sad for quite a different reason. Thus:

1642 Nov 30. POTTER bur Agnes of Dunstable wounded at the batell at Edgehill.
1645 Aug 27. WILLIAMS bur Mr a souldyer of the King's Army was slayne by the Parliament souldyers and buryed the same day.

And what story lies behind the entry for January 11, 1628? It says:

Jan 11 (------) baptised Mary, d of a strange woman who would not acknowledge her name and was buried on the thirteenth of the same month.

But was it the infant or the nameless mother who was buried the day after the baptism?

In May 1701 a man named Blew came from Cosell, Warwicks and married Ellinor Gall of the parish of Little Brickhill. In itself this is unremarkable except that other entries relating to the couple, elsewhere spell the name as Blue, not Blew. And some of the entries supply True as the Christian name. It has to be admitted that the name True Blue sounds almost too good to be believed.

A note of the fly leaf of one of the volumes of the Parish Registers has this note:

'TRUE BLUE was an officer's servant in the Royal Horse Guards – The Blues. His master having been taken prisoner in the Wars he managed to rescue him and in gratitude his master bought his discharge. He came to Little Brickhill and kept the White Lion Inn – then the largest in the town. Perhaps the largest but one. His name was Coles.'
'The above was related to the Reverend G. R. Scobell, Vicar of Bickleigh, South Devon by Richard Miles of this parish on May 12 1882.'

On the left, True Blue's Tomb at Little Brickhill. On the right, the Tomb of the Reverend Edward Jones, Rector of Little Brickhill for fifty-seven years. (JH)

One burial entry concerns no less a person than the Lord of the Manor of Little Brickhill, Sir Pexall Brocas:

> *'1630 Aug 14 BROCAS Sir Pexall, Knight, Lord of ye Manor, dyed August 13 and was buryed in part.'*

'Buryed in part'? That odd phraseology refers to the fact that Sir Pexall was buried twice! Part of him in Little Brickhill, and part of him at Ivinghoe Aston where he was also the landowner.

Sir Pexall Brocas in any age would be considered a 'character'. He was notorious as a womaniser and was said to have sired a hundred children. He spent little of his time living at home. His whereabouts in October 1613 are on record. He was in London where he was brought before the Ecclesiastical Court and found guilty of behaviour so scandalous that he was made to stand for three days, clad in a white penitential gown, on the steps of St. Paul's Cathedral.

Surprisingly, the name Brocas only occurs in the Little Brickhill Registers three times. As well as the burial entry already quoted, there is an earlier entry, in December 1610, relating to the baptism of his daughter Mary. The only other entry concerning Brocas has the distinction of being the longest entry in any of the ten volumes of the Little Brickhill Registers. It deserves to be quoted in full:

'At a Vestrye holden in this Parish Church of Little Brickhill on the third Sunday after Epiphany 1624 it was and is ordered by and with the consent of the right Worthshippefull Sir Pexall Brocas Knight Lord of the Manor here and of Francis Clethero, Vicar, the Churchwardens and other the inhabitants of the said towne as followeth warning being first given in the Church for the meeting of this vestry according to Lawe.

Whereas at this present there is a suite depending in the Ecclesiasticall Court before the right worshippefull John Smith Batchelor of the Lawes, Commissary and Officiall of this Archdeaconry of Buckingham for and concerning a rate of sixteen shillings, foure pence farthing rated and taxed upon the sayd Sir Pexall on the five and twentieth day January Anno Dom 1623 according to the computation of the Church of England for and towards the repayre of the Church, for divers lands which the said Sir Pexall at the time of the making of the said rate did and yet doth hold in his owne occupacion. The which rate the said Sir Pexall refused to pay for that the Ile in the upper end of the Church adioyning unto the Chancell on the south side is deteyned and kept from him and divers persons of mean qualitye permitted to use the same and sitt therein in the time of divine service which Ile as he affirmeth hath of ancient time belonged to the Lords of the said manor of Little Brickhill only and so ought now to appertain unto him being Lord there.

Is now therefore the appeasing and finall determination of the said suite and of all other controversies which may hereafter arise and growe about the taxation of any of the lands which the said Sir Pexall Brocas shall at any time hereafter at the making of any taxe for and towards the repayres of the said Church and Ile to the purpose above agreed and concluded that the said Sir Pexall for his life time and others hereafter succeeding holders of the said Manor shall quietly ....

BUT AT THAT POINT THE REST OF THE PAGE WAS CUT OUT OF THE REGISTER!!

So did Sir Pexall get away with it? Tradition says that he did.

One way or another, the Reverend Francis Clethero, Vicar of the Peculiar Parish of St. Mary Magdalene, Little Brickhill, must have found his most notable parishioner peculiar too!

Chapter 13

BUT ONLY ONE IS GREAT

England has no less than four rivers called the Ouse. Perhaps
this isn't so surprising. After all, the word 'ouse' is from the
Celtic 'uisage' meaning water. Ouse with a small 'o' has an
alternative spelling of 'ouzel', or 'ousel'. Buckinghamshire has
a River Ouzel and it runs into one of England's four River
Ouses, the only one called Great.

The Yorkshire Ouse is formed by the rivers Sware and Ure.
It runs for some sixty miles to join the River Trent on its way to
form the Humber Eastuary in NE England.

The Sussex Ouse is a more modest affair. It rises in the
South Downs and flows across thirty miles of Sussex
countryside before entering the English Channel at Newhaven.

In the Gog Magog hills of Suffolk rises the Little Ouse. It
flows north and west through Norfolk to join the Great Ouse at
the Cambridgeshire border.

The Great Ouse, the only one graced with the adjective
Great, winds its way for over a hundred and seventy miles
from its source at Brackley in Northamptonshire to its final
destination at Kings Lynn and The Wash. This makes it perhaps
the fourth or fifth longest river in England. It twists and turns
passing through the four counties of Northants., Bucks., Beds.
and Cambs., and then, finally joined by the Little Ouse it enters
Norfolk and Suffolk.

It is sometimes called the Bedfordshire Ouse, and that is under-
standable. For nearly fifty miles of its total length the Great Ouse
meanders through Bedfordshire. And in all its length Bedford
is beyond doubt the principal place through which it passes.

The Ouse at Tyringham. The bridge was designed by John Soane who later designed the Bank of England in Threadneedle Street. (JH)

In 1921 Bedford celebrated its millenium. For over a thousand years Bedford and its River Ouse have figured importantly in English history.

Offa was the King of Mercia in the 8th century. He founded St. Cuthbert's Church in Bedford. He died in 796. Tradition says that his body was brought to Bedford where his burial place became a shrine. No trace of the shrine has survived but the authority for this tradition is Matthew Paris, Chief Scribe of St. Alban's Abbey in the reign of Henry III. He wrote:

'Offa's body when brought to the town of Bedeford is said to have been buried in royal manner in a certain Chapel . . . situated within the city on the banks of the River Ouse. But it is reported to this day that the said Chapel becoming ruinous through long use and the violence of that river became submerged and owing to the rapacity of the stream was completely destroyed, along with the actual tomb of the king, or at least as some assert, was hurled in ruins irresistibly into the bed of the river'.

In the 9th century the Danes by their constant raiding had overrun much of eastern England. One of their main invasion routes into mid-Anglia was by way of the Great Ouse, navigable as far as Bedford.

Alfred the Great, King of Wessex, emerged from the Isle of Athelney where he had taken refuge and routed the Danes at the Battle Ethandune in 878. He recognised that the Danes were here to stay. The days when they simply raided and pillaged, and then withdrew, were over. Now they coalesced with the Saxons and settled permanently.

The far-seeing Alfred negotiated with the Danes. Under the Frith or Peace of Wedmore it was agreed that Guthrum the Dane should accept Christian baptism, and that the area totally under his control should be confined to the north and east of an agreed border. In fixing that border between the Danelaw and the Kingdom of Wessex the Great Ouse played its part. 'Let the bounds of our dominion,' decreed Alfred, 'stretch to the River Thames and from thence to the Water of Lea, and then straight into Bedford, and finally along by the River Ouse, let them end at Watling Street.'

The Great Ouse at Bedford. (JH)

The arrangement thus come to held reasonably good for about a century. But in 921 the Danes made four attacks. One Danish force stormed Towcester. It was to repel this attack that the King, Edward the Elder, camped with an army at Passenham just outside Stony Stratford, to deny the Danes the crossing of the Ouse which would have threatened Buckingham.

A second Danish force attacked Wigmore, and a third surrounded Maldon.

Most threatening of all a fourth Danish force occupied Tempsford and advanced via the Ouse to attack Bedford.

Edward the Elder, King Alfred's son, came hotfoot to Bedford from Passenham. With great energy he supervised the development of a defensive position on the banks of the Ouse in Bedford. For a month the work went on. Then came the dreaded news – the Danes in thirty ships were pressing up the Ouse from Tempsford. Soon the ships could be seen and then the sound of the oars in the rowlocks could be heard.

The Danes landed and soon battle was joined between them and the Saxons. The fighting, with spears, battle-axes and swords was furious. The battle swayed backwards and forwards till at last the Danes broke. They fled back to their ships, making a desperate last stand near Howbury. To this day that spot is still called 'Bloody Battle Bridge'.

A week or two later the English attacked the Danish base at Tempsford, destroying it and killing many of its inhabitants.

A century later came the Norman Conquest. To secure his victory William embarked on a considerable programme of castle building all over the country. Initially they were motte and bailey constructions. Many were built in the valley of the Ouse. The remains of three of them are still to be seen in Milton Keynes – at Old Wolverton, Bradwell, and Shenley.

In time many motte and bailey castles were replaced by more elaborate castles. Two of these were erected at Buckingham and at Bedford, thus recognising the strategic importance of the Ouse.

Little is known about Buckingham Castle, but the records show that in 1307 and 1312 Buckingham Castle was listed as one that was to be defended and victualled. And in 1484 Richard III made a grant to John Grey of Wilton 'for the food for the King's hawkes secured upon the Castle and Manor of Buckingham'. Even as late as 1599 old Corporation Records show that there was still a Constable of Buckingham Castle.

The Castle at Bedford was altogether a larger and more important affair. Early in the 13th century it became a rallying point for the Barons who were growing increasingly restive against King John. The King sent forces to seize the castle in 1215. Having done so he gave the castle to the man who had seized it in his name. His successor, Henry III found it necessary to lead an army in person to take the castle back from the man to whom King John had given it.

John Spede in the 16th century wrote thus of this episode:

> 'When the Barons forsook their allegeance to King John the Towne and Castell were rendered up into their hands; and lastly by King Henry the third laid level, even with the ground, some ruinous walles appearing towards the Ouse, but not a stone left upon the Mount where stood his foundations'.

Bedford's greatest literary figure beyond any doubt is John Bunyan. How well he knew the Ouse. He knew it in his childhood at Elstow where he was born. He knew it in his late teens when he served as a Trooper in the Parliamentary Army at Newport Pagnell. As an itinerant tinker, travelling all over the Bedfordshire countryside he learned to know the river in all its moods. And he served part at least of one of his two terms of imprisonment in the jailhouse on the old bridge.

It was in prison that he wrote Pilgrim's Progress. In that allegory he writes of the 'River of the Water of Life'. This is the Ouse in its summer mood, with Christian and his companion walking happily in the riverside meadow. But the sombre river in its winter mood is also there. Then it becomes 'The River of

Death' which must be crossed even though there is no bridge. That river was deep and dangerous but the Pilgrim was told: 'You must go through or you cannot come at the Gate'.

This literary description of the Ouse in its dangerous mood was true to life. In winter the placid, friendly river could become a raging torrent. Matthew Paris, the scribe of St. Albans Abbey, wrote of one fearful flood which happened in 1256:

'About the day of S.Ciriac, November 20, there happened a terrible storm of rain, lightning and thunder. The mill wheels were torn off their axles and dashed with such force against the houses that were near as to break them to pieces, and the wind did the same with the sails of the windmills; the piles of the bridge, hayricks, fishermen's cottages, with their nets and punts, and even the children in their cradles were carried away. Bedford which the river called Use washes underwent irreparable damage. For in one place six houses together were carried away by the rapid floods, their inhabitants being scarcely rescued; and other places near the same river underwent like disaster'.

During the 17th century commercial traffic was still largely dependent on river and sea transport. But great changes were pending. The volume of traffic was increasing at a time when transport by water grew ever more difficult. Many stretches of rivers, formerly useful for transport, grew markedly less so. The growing number of mills, with weirs and dams to provide motive power, made river navigation more and more difficult. Tolls increased the cost of river carriage. Parliament passed a number of Acts aimed at improving river navigation, but these proved insufficient.

The day was coming when transport by road would greatly increase. In time, too, canals would be constructed, and the railways would follow. Such developments would only come in the 19th century. At the very end of that century, the only River Ouse in England to be called Great made one last effort to boost its usefulness. In April 1892 an advertisement appeared in the newspaper:

THE RIVER OUSE NAVIGATION

In One Lot, the above valuable WATERWAY, about 31 miles in length, connecting the towns of Bedford, St. Neots, Huntingdon, and St. Ives with tidal waters, and traversing a thriving agricultural district, having numerous populous villages. There are 13 locks and 16 tolling places, also three freeholds cottage and accommodation lands, the whole forming a very promising commercial investment.'

But the *Daily Telegraph* on 6th April, 1892 carried the following story:

'At Tokenhouse-yard they are in the habit of selling all manner of strange things, but perhaps one of the queerest "lots" that has ever been offered for sale was that which failed to find a purchaser yesterday. This was nothing less than a navigable river. The Ouse, from St. Ives to Bedford, with all rights of levying tolls upon it, was the highly desirable property which lay at the mercy of the highest bidder. It was explained by the auctioneer that the aforesaid rights were of venerable antiquity, and confirmed by ancient Acts of Parliament. Yet in spite of these undeniable attractions, a sum of only £5,200 was offered, and so the river had ultimately to undergo the singular humiliation of being "bought in". Probably no river has ever met such a fate before'.

That embarrassment notwithstanding, the Bedfordshire Ouse is still Great.

As Robert Louis Stevenson once wrote:

'After a good woman, and a good book and tobacco, there is nothing so good as a good river'.

Chapter 14

TRIAL AND ERROR

The year—1171. The place —Bedford. The occasion—A Court Case. The defendant—Ailward. The charge—Theft.

But this was no simple case of petty crime. True, the theft was petty enough. Yet the defendant was ordered to have his eyes put out and to suffer other mutilation.

Stephen's 'Criminal Law in England' gives a full report of the case. In broad outline it tells how Ailward, a Bedford man, was angry because a neighbour who owed him money refused to pay. So Ailward broke into his neighbour's house, while the owner was away at the inn. Ailward contented himself with taking only the door lock, a whetstone, and a few tools.

The neighbour, returning from the inn, learned from his children what had happened. He set off in search of Ailward. When he found him he snatched the whetstone from his hand and hit Ailward over the head with it. He then drew a knife and stabbed Ailward through the arm. Next, he frog-marched Ailward back to the house he had broken into, and imprisoned him there.

He hung the items that had been stolen around Ailward's neck and told the neighbours who had gathered that he was going to 'have the law' on Ailward for being a thief.

But in the crowd was Fulco, and he was an Apparitor, a Court official. And Fulco said: 'Wait a minute. A man cannot be mutilated for stealing goods worth less than a shilling.' Others in the crowd saw the point at once. They hurriedly scratched around to find other items to hang about Ailward's neck as evidence of his thieving. In no time at all, to the few simple tools that Ailward *had* stolen, they added a pellium, a bundle of assorted other items, some linen, and a few garments. And for good measure, they added an iron hoe as well. Fulco said he thought that would do nicely. So they all carried Ailward, draped rather like a scarecrow, to the Court.

The case was heard by Richard the Sheriff and other knights. Ailward was found guilty but the Court decided to postpone the announcement of the sentence for a month. Ailward spent that month in gaol in Bedford.

The month being over, the case came back to Court again. But this time the Court sat in Leighton Buzzard. When the hearing began Ailward demanded the right to have the case settled by his taking on Fulco in single combat. Alternatively, he offered to prove his innocence by undergoing 'the ordeal of fire'. Fulco objected to both these proposals. He suggested instead that Ailward should submit to the 'ordeal of water'.

No decision was reached that day, and the wretched Ailward was taken back to Bedford where he spent another month in gaol. When the Court sat again, sentence was passed. It was ordered that Ailward should have his eyes put out, and that he should suffer other mutilation also, and that 'his members should be buried in the earth in the presence of a multitude of people'.

Thus far, this true tale, grim as it is, merely reflects the

'Ordeal by Water' was demanded for a 12th century thief in Bedford. But instead they put out his eyes.

customs and standards of its age. Its recital in Stephen's 'Criminal Law of England' presumably testifies to its accuracy.

But there is a strange corollary to the tale. Ailward's offence, and his fate, belong to the year 1171. That was one year after the murder of Archbishop Thomas à Becket in Canterbury Cathedral. That murder shocked the nation, and instantly Becket became a figure of veneration. Stories began to be told of miracles being performed by the murdered saintly Archbishop.

Professor Froude researched the death of Archbishop Becket, and studied the ways in which the public reacted. One reaction was that the murder in Canterbury Cathedral began to be depicted in mural paintings in churches. The Parish Church of Winslow is one example.

But what most vividly illustrated the intense and widespread reaction of the nation was the accumulation of folk tales, and the claims of miracles wrought by Archbishop Becket.

Becket was murdered in 1170. By 1173 he had already been officially canonised. His tomb in the Cathedral became an instant shrine to which pilgrims flocked not only from all parts of this country, but from abroad as well.

The King, Henry II, had caused Becket's death by his petulant outburst – 'Who will rid me of this troublesome priest'. King Henry himself went to do penance at Becket's shrine.

Professor Froude in his account of the martyrdom of St. Thomas of Canterbury quotes examples of the miracles attributed to the martyr. The story of what happened to Ailward as related in Stephen's 'Criminal Law in England' is given an astonishing new twist in one of the miracle stories that Professor Froude collected. He sets it out as follows:

While Ailward was in prison a priest counselled him a penance of five floggings each day, and to entrust his cause to the Virgin, and especially to the martyr St. Thomas of Canterbury. At the end of a month Ailward was brought before the justiciars at Leighton Buzzard,

*Canterbury Cathedral where Becket was murdered in 1170.
Did he perform miracles in Bedford? (JH)*

where the constable appeared to prosecute, and Ailward had appealed for a wager of battle, or for the ordeal of the hot iron. These the judges refused, and the penalty for felony being loss of eyes and further mutilation, Ailward was delivered to the knife'.

Thus far, this all agrees with the account in Stephen's Criminal Law in England'. It is from this point onwards that folklore takes over. The story collected by Froude continues:

'A neighbour took him into his house and dressed the wounds, which began to heal. On the twelfth night St. Thomas had come to his bedside and told him that if he presented himself the next day, with a candle, at the altar of the Virgin in Bedford Church, and did not doubt in his heart that God was able and willing to cure him, his eyes would be restored. Next day he had told his vision to the dean of St. Paul's Church in Bedford who had gone with him to the altar of St. Paul's, the townspeople crowding in to see the promised miracle. There at the altar he prayed and believed. The bandages had been taken from the empty eye-sockets, and in the hollows two small glittering spots the size of birds' eyes could be seen, and Ailward could see. Ailward had gone on pilgrimage to offer thanks at the shrine of the martyr. The Mayor and Corporation of Bedford had sent witnesses who had deposed to the completeness of the mutilation beyond all doubts'.

Professor Froude, in his research, apparently came across this story in the writings of Nigellus, a Canterbury monk, who wrote it at a time when Becket's death was fresh in the minds of everyone.

Trial and Error. About the Trial there is no doubt. For the 20th century reader, Error was there too in the horrendous cruelty of the punishment. Whether there was further Error in the seeming miracle must be left to each person's credulity.

Chapter 15

MONEY MATTERS

(Especially if you are short of it!)

Surprisingly often coins continue to be found in the ground dating back to the Roman period. Browne Willis, Lord of the Manors of Bletchley and Fenny Stratford, was an expert on coinage. His Note Books list first century coins of the Emperors Claudius and Nero.

Coins were uncovered at Magiovinium, the Roman settlement near Fenny Stratford, and at Galley Hill near Stony Stratford. The Galley Hill find comprised about three hundred Roman silver coins.

In 1849 a sensational discovery unearthed many hundreds of gold coins near Great Horwood. What excited people so much about these coins was the fact that they were all of a date *before* the Roman occupation. It is thought they represented the wealth of a chief who hid them because the Roman invasion had started.

Coinage had been introduced into Britain by the Belgae in the first century BC. When the Romans invaded opposition to them in the east of England and in mid-Anglia was led by the Catevellauni tribe. The King of the Catevellauni was Cunobelinus who had his headquarters at Colchester. His son was Caractacus (also known as Caradoc). He was taken captive to Rome. But the Catevellauni reached an uneasy compromise with the Romans. It was said that Cunobelinus styled himself as Rex Brittanicus and that he minted his own coins bearing that title. Shakespeare's play, Cymbeline, is a highly fanciful account of him.

We owe the units of pounds, shillings and pence (LSD) to the Romans. For them the pound, Libra, was divided into shillings, Solidi, and shillings were divided into pence, Denarii. This division, comprising twelve pence to the shilling, and twenty shillings to the pound, stayed with us from the Roman occupation until our conversion to decimal currency some nineteen centuries later.

The Romans left in the fifth century. By 600AD silver coins called sceats were minted. In Offa's reign (757–796) the silver penny was introduced and remained the main coin in circulation until gold coins were re-introduced in the 14th century.

When an uneasy peace between the Danes and English was achieved in the Treaty of Wedmore in 878, 'market forces' established an exchange rate. For the Danes in the Danelaw the unit of currency was the mark. For some time the mark was reckoned to be worth 128 silver pennies. Later the exchange rate became 160.

Half-pennies first appeared in the 9th century and survived until 1969. In 1279 farthings were minted and they survived until 1961.

It was obviously vital that the king should control the minting of coinage. With the silver penny for so long the standard coin in England, the practice was introduced that the dies for the penny would be produced centrally – at the Royal Mint. It was Athelstan in 928 who regulated coining in this way. Originally the Royal Mint was at the Tower of London. (It transferred in 1811 to Tower Hill and in 1968 to Llantrisant in South Wales.)

The dies for the silver penny, produced at the Royal Mint, could then be sent to Mints at various places for local production of coins. Naturally such work could only be entrusted to fortified places which already possessed markets. Bedford qualified on both counts. The key figure in the process was called a 'moneyer'. He was supplied with the dies and was authorised to mint coins locally in Bedford, adding his own name, and that of Bedford, to the minted coin. It is interesting to notice in the list of successive moneyers at Bedford three Danish names, Grim, Gunni, and Ulcetel.

It was also possible that a dishonest moneyer could profit by using debased silver and by making the coins short in weight. Many succumbed to this temptation – rather foolishly, bearing in mind that their own names had to be stamped on the coins. In 1125 Henry I summoned all the moneyers to Winchester and offenders were weeded out. The Bedford moneyer then was Edric. The penalties for malpractice could not have been more draconian – the loss of the right hand, and castration!

Another threat to sound money was clipping. As silver coins really were made of silver, the temptation was great to clip a little off from the edges of coins. Clippings, even of minute size, could be accumulated and melted down. This practice had become fairly widespread by the middle of the 12th century.

Another problem was how to give change, when all coins were either gold or silver. Clearly it could not be done by cutting up the coins! So tokens were introduced. Merchants and traders devised their own tokens, bearing their own names and designs. Tokens were not coins in any technical sense, but they served the same purpose nevertheless. In Bedford William Faldo issued tokens in 1659. William Isaac, who later became Mayor, did the same in 1666.

As at Bedford, so also at Dunstable, Potton, Leighton Buzzard, Luton, Buckingham, Stony Stratford and other places, merchants and traders devised and issued their own tokens. Even quite small villages got in on the act. Tokens are known to have been issued at Barton, Clifton, Wilden, Husborne Crawley, Shillington and Shefford.

Such traders' tokens continued to be produced and issued until 1672. In that year the Royal Mint itself began to mint copper coins. From that moment onwards traders' tokens were suppressed.

Browne Willis, who was an antiquarian and historian, as well as being the Lord of three Manors and a great church builder and benefactor, made a great collection of Trade Tokens. He catalogued them all and built cabinets for them, and then presented the entire collection to Oxford University.

New denominations of coins appeared in the reigns of successive kings. Edward III issued gold Nobles. Henry VI introduced Angels (worth 6s 8d). The gold pound worth 240 pence first appeared in 1489. Crowns and Half-crowns were first minted in 1526.

It was Henry VIII who first minted silver shillings. The golden pound was first named as a Sovereign in 1816. It became the standard unit of currency. As such it replaced the Guinea which was valued as 21s and had served as the basis of currency from 1717 until 1816.

Gold sovereigns and Half-sovereigns really were gold. They ceased to be minted in 1917. Silver coins ceased to be largely silver in 1921. From 1947 onwards coins have been cupro-nickel.

Sending it Out and Getting it Back

Monarchs and governments, as well as jealously guarding their powers of controlling the minting of money, were also concerned to get back the money in circulation by means of taxes! Benjamin Franklin once said:

"In this world nothing can be said to be certain except death and taxes!'

In 1222 for the first time a tax was introduced called the Poll Tax. The name derives from the German word 'polle' meaning 'head'. In a sense it was a tax for just existing. It was the later attempts to enforce a Poll Tax in 1377, 1379 and 1381 that led to the violent opposition called The Peasants' Revolt in 1381. The Tax was then abandoned.

From 1290 onwards personal taxes on property were introduced. Taxes were assessed by officials county by county.

Bletchley, Water Eaton and Fenny Stratford were jointly assessed at £12 per annum. Only Aylesbury was assessed at a higher rate than this. The tax figure for a place having been assessed, the finding of that amount was then looked for from the local landowners. Henry de Grey, the Lord of the Manor, had to furnish about eleven shillings of the £12. The rest came from about seventy other lesser landowners in smaller amounts.

But Poll Taxes and Land Taxes were never enough to produce the revenue needed. So over the centuries a range of other taxes were introduced. Excise taxes on goods first appeared in 1643. In one form or another they have remained with us ever since. It was the tax on tea which provoked the incident of The Boston Tea Party, the signal for the revolt of the American Colonies.

Equally disastrous was the Ship Tax introduced by Charles I. Originally it was only imposed on coastal areas but was then extended to inland areas as well. John Hampden of Buckinghamshire led the opposition to it. That opposition was a precursor of the Civil War which brought the execution of the king and the eleven year rule of England as a republic under Oliver Cromwell.

After the restoration of the monarchy under Charles II in 1660, the need for increased national revenue prompted the introduction of the bizarre Hearth Tax in 1662, levied at the rate of 2s on every fire hearth. It was naturally much resented but it remained on the Statute Book from 1662 to 1689.

Its place was taken in 1696 by the even more bizarre Window Tax. That survived until 1851, but it was partially evaded by householders who reduced their liability by bricking up some of their windows. The effects of this are still everywhere visible.

In 1799 came the first Income Tax. It started at two shillings in the pound. Britain was then at war with Napoleon. On introducing Income Tax Pitt said it was a temporary imposition made necessary by the war. But nobody thought to remove it when that war ended. In a variety of forms it has remained with us ever since – a major source of revenue.

Viscount Sherbrooke, speaking in the House of Commons in April 1870 was being sardonic when he said:

'The Chancellor of the Exchequer is a man whose duties make him more or less of a taxing machine. He is intrusted with a certain amount of misery which it is his duty to distribute as fairly as he can'.

The original Poll Tax had been a tax just for living. In 1894 the Finance Act introduced a tax also for dying! Death Duties were a tax on the capital value of assets owned by a person at his or her death. It has been revised in various ways since then. In 1986 it took its present form as an Inheritance Tax.

Money matters. Indeed it does! Even this brief survey has shown how many and diverse are the ways in which money touches the life (and death) of every individual.

In his play, 'Major Barbara', Bernard Shaw wrote:

'The universal regard for money is the one hopeful fact in our civilisation, the one sound spot in our social conscience. Money is the most important thing in the world. It represents health, strength, honour, generosity, and beauty as conspicuously as the want of it represents illness, weakness, disgrace, meanness and ugliness'.

Chapter 16

THE RISE AND FALL OF SALDEN

At the Court of William I in London, after the Conqueror had been crowned, a knight named Richard Fortescue served as 'Cupp Bearer' to the monarch.

Richard Fortescue's descendants continued in royal employ for the next nine generations. One of them, Sir John Fortescue, was made Governor of Brie in France under Henry V. Another was a Knight Banneret to Henry VII. Yet another, Sir Adrian Fortescue, was a Gentleman of the Privy Council to Henry VIII. But Henry executed him for treason in 1539!

Sir Adrian Fortescue's son was Sir John Fortescue, 'Knight, Chancellor of the Exchequer and of the Duchy of Lancaster, Master of the Wardrobe and of the Privy Council'. All these high offices he held in the reign of Elizabeth I whose second cousin he was.

Sir John Fortescue was much of an age with Elizabeth. When she ascended the throne in 1558 she already knew his worth for he had been her tutor for many years. Once Queen, she appointed him Keeper of the Great Wardrobe and 'trusted him with both the ornaments of her soul and body'. Elizabeth's promotion of John Fortescue thus made amends for the fact that her father had executed his father!

John Fortescue became MP for Buckinghamshire and served in Parliament for forty years. His wealth increased enormously – every office brought rich perquisites as well as salary. He set about acquiring a place in the country where he could build a house befitting his high place in society.

In 1565 he bought the Manor of Salden near the village of

Sir John Fortescue, cousin to Elizabeth I. His monument in Little Horwood Church. (NK)

Mursely, about four miles from Bletchley. Salden was an ancient Manor. At the Conquest it had been awarded to Lewin de Newenham. Subsequently it had been owned by the Fitz-Neales and the Fitz-Geralds. As early as 1253 there is record of a Chantry Chapel at Salden to the honour of St. Nicholas.

John Fortescue set to work to build a new house on the site of the one he had bought in 1565. By about 1580 it was complete. The new Salden Manor was immense – a palace rather than a Manor House. It cost about £33,000 to build – a sum approaching a million in today's money.

With Salden Manor went its land. But John Fortescue wanted more. In 1571 he bought the land belonging to the dissolved Snelshall Priory. Seven years later he also acquired the three manors of Shenley, Winslow and Drayton Parslow.

While these purchases were being made the building of Salden House went ahead. Its front elevation was nearly sixty yards long, and fronted a court or square. The 'palace' – for such it could be described – was of three stories. In the middle storey was a gallery nearly one hundred and fifty feet long. The whole building was topped by a balustrade.

But Salden's most notable feature was the use it made of windows. Each of the three floors had symmetrical rows of them, ten in each row. Many of these windows were enriched with coats-of-arms in stained glass. Within the house were alabaster or marble chimney-pieces. On the roof-ridge a line of chimneys protruded, some single, some in pairs, and other in threes.

The whole building was described as being 'of excellent masonry in the brick and stone work'. Fortunately for John Fortescue he was building this magnificent edifice in an area rich in the clay needed for brickmaking. Indeed, tiles, pottery and bricks have been made in North Bucks since Roman Times.

To meet Fortescue's needs, more and more brick clamps were set up – at least a dozen of them. So the magnificent Salden Mansion was completed. Life in the great house was appropriately on the grand scale. Some sixty servants worked there. One of them was solely occupied in opening and closing

Fortescue's palatial mansion at Salden. No trace of it remains.

the windows and shutters each day!

There was a butcher and a baker and, it is said, a bullock a day was killed. In the summer the butter was put to cool in a fountain or spring of water. Large cisterns existed for receiving and preserving fish, reared in a nearby 'large piece of water'. Each day household food-remains were distributed to the poor and needy.

And royalty came to stay. Queen Elizabeth visited, probably more than once. So too did her successor, King James I. He came, with his Queen, in 1603, the very first year of his reign. During that visit he created twenty-two new knights at a ceremony in the great hall on 28 June.

Thus far, the connections between royalty and the Fortescues had been uniformly fruitful – save for that one 'hiccup' when Henry VIII had executed Sir Adrian Fortescue in 1559, because of the Fortescue connection with Anne Boleyn. There was stained glass evidence of that connection as we shall see in a moment.

But the time was to come when Fortescue relations with the monarch would cause problems. That time came in the Civil War when Sir John Fortescue declared for King Charles against Parliament.

In May 1644 Sir John Fortescue was taken prisoner at Islip. He remained a prisoner until 1659. He had by this time become a Catholic. The victorious Roundheads confiscated his property at Drayton Parslow and at Mursley. His Manor at Stewkley was sequestered as a penalty for recusancy (adherence to the Catholic faith).

When estates were confiscated and sequestered it was possible to 'compound' for them and to recover them – but at a price. The recovery of the Fortescue manors was an enormous strain on the Fortescue finances.

Sir John was finally released from prison in 1659. By then the rule of Cromwell was all but over. Next year, 1660, Charles II was restored to the throne of his executed father.

At the Restoration a vast amount of sorting out had to be tackled. An Act of Indemnity and Oblivion was passed. Broadly speaking, its aim was to forgive everyone – except the Regicides who had signed the Death Warrant of Charles I. All lands confiscated by either side in the Civil War were to be restored to their owners. Even so, many leading families, restored to their estates, found themselves almost bankrupt.

This, then, is the background against which we have to view the decline of the Fortescue family finances. (They must have been made the more parlous, too, by the much resented Hearth Tax which was introduced in 1662, given the great number of chimneys which graced Salden's roof-ridge.)

Up with the Rocket – Down with the Stick

From the days of the Conquest up to the 17th century the Fortescues had gone from strength to strength. They reached their apogee in the person and ambitions of Sir John Fortescue, the builder of Salden Manor. His creation of that splendid house was the outward manifestation of his status and success. His rocket had soared high into the heavens and shone there gloriously. But the dazzle days of Salden were all but over. Soon the stick which had carried the rocket into the heavens would fall to earth.

The Fortescue title became extinct finally in 1729. But long before then the various properties had been divided and sold. In 1738 the melancholy demolition of the great Salden Mansion began. By 1743 it was complete. Salden House was no more. Today only a farmhouse marks the site.

For thirty shillings Browne Willis bought the stained glass windows with the coats-of-arms. Some of these he incorporated

The Salden Window in St. Martin's Church, Fenny Stratford. (NK)

in the parlour of his own house, Whaddon Hall. But others he incorporated in a window at the east end of the new St. Martin's Church he had recently built in Fenny Stratford. That window is still there in St. Martin's Church, though no longer at the east end. It is now in the north-west corner of the building.

At the foot of the right hand light of that window can clearly be seen the Fortescue coat-of-arms and the name of Anne Boleyn. The family connection of the Fortescues with Anne Boleyn had made John Fortescue second cousin once removed to Queen Elizabeth and must have contributed to the rise to high office of John Fortescue.

But it had earlier cost the life of Sir Adrian Fortescue, John's father, executed by Henry VIII who had also executed Anne Boleyn herself. So Anne takes her sad place in the story of the Rise and Fall of Salden Manor.

Chapter 17

TRAVELLERS TALES

'St. Albans is the capital town, though not the county town of Hertfordshire. It has a great corn market, and is famous for its ancient church, built on the ruins, or part of the ruins of the most famous Abbey of Verulam, the greatness of which is to be judged by the old walls, which one sees for a mile before we come to town'.

It was Daniel Defoe who wrote that in 1724, he who wrote *Robinson Crusoe*. His account continues:

'In this church as some workmen were digging for the repairs of the church, they found some steps which led to a door in a very thick stone wall, which being opened, there was discovered an arched stone vault, and in the middle of it a large coffin near 7 foot long, which being opened, there was in it the corpse of a man, the flesh was not consumed but discoloured; by the arms and other paintings of the wall, it appeared that this must be the body of Humphry Duke of Gloucester, commonly called the Good Duke of Gloucester, one of the sons of Henry IV, and brother to King Henry V, and by the most indisputable authority, must have lain buried there these 277 years'.

Defoe's arithmetic was absolutely correct. Duke Humphrey died in 1447. He earned the title of 'Good' for his patronage of learning. When Henry VI came to the throne he was a minor, so Humphrey shared with his brother, John of Lancaster, the Protectorship of the young king. But Humphrey was caught up in a bitter feud with his uncle, Henry Beaufort, Bishop of Winchester. He was arrested and accused of treason in 1447 but died that year before his trial, and so came to be buried in that seven foot coffin of which Defoe wrote.

Daniel Defoe was born in London in 1660, in the same year as the Restoration of Charles II to the throne. He was the son of James Foe, a tallow-chandler. Daniel changed the name from Foe to Defoe when he was thirty-five. He had once intended to be a Presbyterian minister but changed his mind and instead became a successful merchant. He had a brief spell as a soldier during Monmouth's Rebellion. Between 1697 and 1714 he served as a spy for William III.

He also took to writing. His success with 'Robinson Crusoe' was followed by 'Moll Flanders'. Then, between 1724 and 1726, he published the three volumes of 'A Tour through the Whole Island of Great Britain'. He died on 24th April 1731.

It is in the second volume that he wrote of St. Albans and the discovery of Duke Humphrey's coffin. He had arrived at St. Albans by way of Bushy Heath, which he found 'a very agreeable prospect'.

'I cannot but remember, with some satisfaction, that having two foreign gentlemen in my company, in our passing over this heath, I say, I could not but then observe, and now remember it with satisfaction, how they were surprised at the beauty of this prospect, and how they looked at one another, and then again turning their eyes every way in a kind of wonder, one of them said to the other, that England was not like other countries, but it was all a planted garden.They had there on the right hand the town of St. Albans in their view; and all the spaces between, and further beyond it, looked indeed like a garden. The enclosed cornfields made one grand parterre, the thick planted hedgerows, like a wilderness or labyrinth, divided in espaliers; the villages interspersed, looked like so many noble seats of gentlemen at a distance. In a word, it was all nature and yet looked like art'.

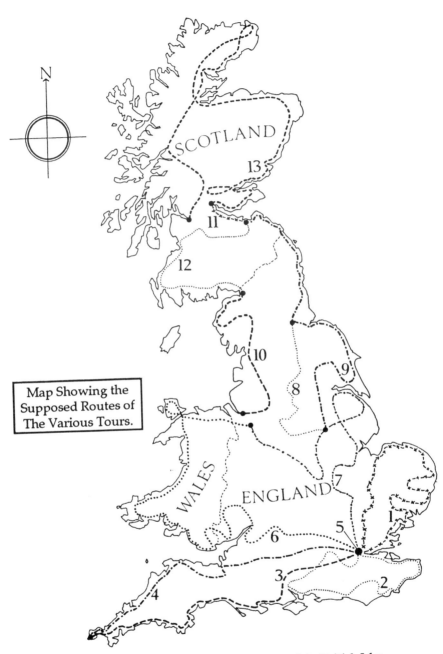

Map Showing the
Supposed Routes of
The Various Tours.

Daniel Defoe's Tours took him to every part of the British Isles.

On another journey Defoe visited Aylesbury and the Vale of Aylesbury. He called it 'a large tract of the richest land in England' and added that he considered it to have 'the richest graziers in England'.

He also visited Northampton, 'the handsomest and best built town in all this part of England'. He considers it 'owes its beauty to its own disasters—' for it was so effectively and suddenly burnt down, that very few houses were left standing; 'tis now finely rebuilt with brick and stone, and the streets made spacious and wide'.

From Northampton he went north to Harborough, over 'deep, dismal roads, the dirtiest and worst in all that part of the country'. He chided the inhabitants of Lutterworth for their ignorance of one of their most famous sons:

> 'Curiosity turned us west to see an old town called Lutterworth, famous for being the birthplace of honest John Wickliff, the first preacher of the Reformation in England . . . yet the people did not so much as know that this great man was born among them'.

Defoe found Bedford 'large, populous and thriving, a pleasant, well-built place, full of very good inns – we found very good entertainment here'.

> 'Here is also the best market for all sorts of provisions that is to be seen in any country town in all these parts of England. Though it is so far from London, yet the higglers or carriers buy great quantities of provisions here for London markets; Also here is a very good trade down the river to Lynn'.

The map of Defoe's tours make it clear that he really did cover 'the Whole Island of Great Britain' – England, Wales, Scotland, and in so doing gives us 'snapshots' of how one observant traveller saw our towns and countryside 270 years ago. (For his comments on the Roads and Turnpikes of his day, see Chapter 18.)

'And So To Bed'

Defoe wrote his 'tours' intending them to be published and bought. A contemporary of his was also putting pen to paper, but his motive was quite different. He was Samuel Pepys who was born in 1633 and died in 1703. He was a Civil Servant, Secretary to the Admiralty. His writing took the form of his famous diary, written between 1660 to 1669. He stopped in that latter year because by then he was almost blind.

Pepys was *not* writing for publication. His Diary was strictly private. Indeed, on occasions he forsook ordinary spelling and took to a cryptic kind of shorthand. This was whenever he wanted to record his naughtier thoughts, or describe his naughtier behaviour. The Diaries, including the enciphered passages, were kept at Magdalene College in Cambridge until 1825 when they were deciphered and edited.

Samuel Pepys had been born at Brampton near Huntingdon and his father still lived there while Samuel was making a name for himself in the capital. Samuel visited Brampton from time to time, and always broke his journey at Bishop's Stortford. When his father died Samuel inherited the family property and installed his sisters in the family home.

The entries in the Diary relating to his journies to Brampton via Bishop's Stortford make interesting reading.

Samuel Pepys. He used a sort of shorthand to cover the naughtier entries in dis diaries.

'*7 October 1667. Up betimes, and did do several things towards settling all matters, both of house and office, in*

*order for my journey to Brampton this day; and so, about
9 a'clock, I and my wife and Willett set out in a coach I
have hired, with 4 horses, and W.Hewer and Murford
rode by us on horseback; and so my wife and she in their
morning gowns, very handsome and pretty and to my
great liking, we set out; and so out at Allgate and so to
the Greenman; and very merry, my wife and girl and I
talking and telling tales and singing; and before night did
come to Bishop Stafford, to the Raynedeere – where Mrs
Aynsworth (who lived heretofore at Cambridge and
whom I knew better than they think for doth live – it was
the woman that, among other things, was great with my
Cosen Barmston of Cottenham, and did use to sing to
him and did teach me "Full forty times over", a very
lewd song) doth live, a woman they are very well
acquainted with, and is here what she was at Cambridge,
and all the goodfellows of the country come hither. We to
supper and we to bed, my wife and I in one bed and the
girl in another in the same room. And lay very well, but
there was so much tearing company in the house, that we
could not see my landlady, so I had no opportunity of
renewing my old acquaintance with her'.*

Reading between the lines, we can easily deduce that Mrs
Aynsworth was a lady of very easy virtue, and that Pepys had
'known' her in more ways than one when she lived at
Cambridge. But on this visit to Bishop's Stortford in 1667 Pepys
had no opportunity to renew his 'knowledge' of her.

Pepys had occasion to go to Brampton again the following
year, and once more he broke his journey at Bishop's Stortford.

*'23 May 1668. Up by 4 a'clock and getting my things
ready and recommending the care of my house to
W.Hewer, I with the boy Tom to The Bull in Bishopsgate
Street and there about 6 took coach, and so away to
Bishops Stafford, and there dined and changed horses and
coach at Mrs Aynsworth's; but I took no knowledge of*

.

her. *Here I hear Mrs Aynsworth is going to live at London; but I believe will be mistaken in it, for it will be found better for her to be chief where she is than to have little to do at London, there being many finer than she there'.*

Three days later the return journey is made, from Brampton back to London. There is the usual stopover at Bishop's Stortford, but there is a difference:

'26 May 1668 . . . About noon came to Bishops Stafford to another house than what we were at the other day, and better used; and here I paid for the reckoning 11s, we dining all together and pretty merry. And then set out again, sleeping most part of the way, and got to Bishopsgate Street before 8 a'clock'.

Did Mrs Aynsworth move to London to face the greater competition there from other ladies of easy virtue? We shall never know. She doesn't reappear in the Diary.

In that same year, 1668, Pepys visited other places in mid-Anglia, among them Buckingham, Newport Pagnell and Bedford. Of Bedford he wrote in his Diary:

'Through pleasant country to Bedford; I ride through the town and a good county town, and there drank one shilling'.

In all probability that was at The Swan, near the old bridge over the Ouse, about which he wrote that it was 'as fine a sight as ever I did see'.

'Ride a Cock Horse'
In his praise of Bedford Pepys was anticipating by about twenty years the approval given to Bedford by an even more remarkable traveller. She was Celia Fiennes, born in 1662, the grand-daughter of Lord Saye and Sele of Broughton Castle.

In her twenties this astonishing young lady rode all over England, side-saddle, visiting literally every county. Like Pepys, she too kept a diary and so we have her observations on life and places in the latter part of the 17th century.

If Pepys is immortalised in the phrase he used so often in his diary – 'And so to bed' – Celia has been immortalised in a popular jingle. As quoted, it runs:

> 'Ride a Cock Horse to Banbury Cross,
> to see a fine lady upon a white horse'.

But the original of the jingle had the line:

> 'to see a FIENNES lady upon a white horse'.

That Fiennes lady wrote of Bedford and its river:

> 'Thence to Bedford Town . . . washed by the river Ouse . . . it runns by a ground which is made into a fine bowling green . . . well kept with seates and summer houses in it for the use of the Town and Country Gentlemen of which many resort to it especially the Market dayes'.

Aylesbury, Buckingham, Great Horwood, Northampton, Woburn, Dunstable, Leighton Buzzard, St. Albans, Stony Stratford, Winslow and Aspley Guise – all of them were visited and commented on by the intrepid Celia.

Her diary was never published until 1888, when a short version of it appeared with the delicious title:

> 'Through England on a Side Saddle in the Time of William and Mary'.

Chapter 18

WHEN THE ROADS
TOOK THEIR TOLL

Who was the cynic who said: 'There's a problem to every answer'? The history of roads and road transport lends support to the idea. The Romans left us a magnificent network of fine roads. When they left we let them deteriorate. When, after many centuries, towns began to grow and trade developed, roads became a major problem. Rivers and streams had often to be crossed by fords rather than by bridges. Even the great Watling Street had its notorious stretches. Celia Fiennes in the 17th century wrote:

> 'From thence we came to Dunstable over a sad road called Hockley in the Hole (Hockliffe) as full of deep sloes (sloughs) in the winter it must be impassable; there is a very good pitch's Causey for foot people and horses that is raised up high from the Roade'.

If blackspots like that were a hazard on such trunk roads as the Watling Street, it was even worse on lesser roads:

> 'The bye roads of Bucks. are extremely bad . . . they have ruts so deep that when the wheels of the chaise fall into them . . . the horse and chaise must inevitably fall into bogs. Finding the way from Fenny Stratford to Whaddon through Water Eaton was such that without a guide I could not have surmounted it . . . had it not been for a

colony of gypsies I might have been obliged to have taken refuge in a milking-house for a night's lodging'.

So wrote a traveller in 1810.

Something had to be done about the roads. For a long time the solution was thought to be to borrow the idea from the old jingle:

'If each before his own door swept, the village would be clean'.

In other words, let each village and town be responsible for the maintenance of the roads which passed through them. But there were problems aplenty in that answer.

To begin with, in many areas there were simply no easily available road-making materials. And who should be responsible for the longer stretches between towns and villages? What sanctions could be applied to villages which botched or neglected their stretches of road?

Local expertise would often be incapable of dealing with such problems as bridging streams and rivers. Floods frequently compounded the problem. In 1725 it was recorded in Bletchley Parish Register:

'June 6th Day. There was a Great Flood at Water Eaton that was so Big that the Like hath not bin seen by all Mens knolidge this four Hundren year be fore'.

That was obviously an exceptionally large flood. But in fact floods cut off Water Eaton from Fenny Stratford and Bletchley almost every year, as Cole's Bletchley Diary testifies. Newport Pagnell, Stony Stratford, Olney, Bedford – all had their stories of horrendous floods, often accompanied by loss of life.

A Statute Labour Act of 1669 attempted to tackle some of the problems of roads. It decreed that farmers and landowners should be responsible for providing six days unpaid labour annually for the upkeep of roads passing through their areas. Justices of the Peace were made responsible for bridges and were given power to levy a rate for the purpose. But it really didn't work. There was no standard of repair, no administrative machinery, and no skilled supervision. A locally appointed 'Overguard of the Highway' was expected to supervise, but he seldom had any real qualification for the job.

The book-keeping side of it all was haphazard to say the least. The 1693 Highway Accounts in Stony Stratford are frank, if not efficient. 'Whenever the Overguard of the Highways or the Treasurer couldn't balance the books they added such items as: "Required to make both sides equal".' In the same Accounts we find.

'April 1697 Money lost by having two guineas of the Town money in my hand when too full 16s.
Dec. 6, 1704 Spent at ye Globe with ye neighbours 1s.'

That latter item suggests that contracts for a week's work were often sealed with beer.

By the second half of the 17th century private and stage coaches proliferated. The parishes bordering the main roads used by the coaches found that the increasing wear and tear had made their duty to maintain the roads well nigh impossible.

As early as 1662 Parliament debated: 'A Bill for Repairing and Maintaining of the Highway called Watling Street in the County of Bedford'. As a result, a Committee of thirty-five members was appointed to deal with the matter. The Committee never reported, because Parliament was prorogued before it could complete its deliberations.

A similar 'Bill for Repairing the Highways of the Counties of Beds., Bucks., Northants., and Warwicks.,' was refused a second reading. It so happened that at that moment Parliament was more preoccupied with water transport than with roads.

But in 1663 a new concept was introduced. It was recognised that leaving road maintenance to the parishes simply was not working. What was the alternative? In 1663 the first Turnpike Act was passed. It dealt only with part of the Great North Road.

For the first time the principle was established that travellers and commerce should contribute towards the cost of road repairs. Justices of the Peace were now given power to raise Tolls to supplement Statutory Work on particular stretches of the highway where heavy wagons had ruined part of the Great North Road. Several similar Acts followed, relating to certain other nominated roads.

Turnpikes needed Toll Houses. This one at Dorchester later became an architect's office. (JH)

But it was in 1706 that a Turnpike Act was passed which for the first time took away from Justices of the Peace the right to raise Tolls, and gave that right to Trustees elected specially for the purpose. This significant new development was specifically related to the Watling Street. The Preamble to that Act said:

'Whereas . . . Watling Street now, and for many years the common post road towards Ireland, is a very ruinous and almost impassable for above eight miles from a place called Fornhill about one mile beyond Hockley and Stoney Stratford . . that it is become dangerous to all

*persons that pass those ways and the ordinary course of
the Laws is not sufficient . . . (several parishes being
unable to repair the road) . . . there being no materials for
the amendment thereof to be had but at a great distance
from the said respective places'.*

Before we look to see how effective that 1706 Turnpike Act
was, it is interesting to read what Daniel Defoe wrote in his
'Tour Through the Whole Island of Great Britain':

*'Suppose you take the other northern road, namely by St.
Albans, Dunstable, Hockley, Newport Pagnell,
Northampton . . . On this road after you are passed
Dunstable . . . you enter the deep clays, which are so
surprisingly soft that it is perfectly frightful to travellers,
and it has been the wonder of foreigners, how,
considering the great numbers of carriages which are
continually passing with heavy loads, those ways have
been made practicable . . .*

*Upon this great road there are wonderful improvements
made and making which no traveller can miss the
observations of, especially if he knew the condition these
ways were formerly in . . .*

*The country set about the work in great earnest and we
now see the most dismal piece of ground for travelling
that ever was in England, handsomely repaired, namely
from the top of the chalky hill beyond Dunstable down in
to Hockley Lane and thro' Hockley, justly called Hockley
in the Hole . . .'*

That was Defoe, writing in 1720. Clearly he approved of
what the 1706 Turnpike Act had achieved. But it hadn't all gone
smoothly. A further Act had been needed in 1709 to deal with
debts contracted by the high cost of buying stone, gravel, wood
and other materials. The power to raise tolls was extended for a
further nine years.

Trustees were empowered to erect gates or turnpikes across any part of the road. A scale of charges was laid down for all users of the road. Collectors and Surveyors were appointed and were required to give account on the first Tuesday of every month and to pay over to the Trustees any surplus.

No less than thirty-two Trustees were appointed – a large number so as to make sure that there would always be a quorum of seven at each meeting. Any nine of the Trustees (two more than the statutory quorum of seven) were empowered to mortgage the tolls provided they gave two weeks notice of their intention to do so at Winslow, Stony Stratford and Woburn. Money raised in that way must be used to discharge any outstanding debts, and to effect further improvement to the road.

Despite the undoubted success of the Turnpike Trust, and the praise heaped on it by Daniel Defoe, soon after the Trustees' tenure ran out in 1736, a new Turnpike Act was needed in 1740:

'By reason of many carriages passing, the road is become very ruinous and bad that horsemen, coaches, waggons and other carriages cannot pass especially in the winter season without danger'.

This time eighty-five Trustees were appointed but the quorum was reduced to five. In the new scale of charges, coaches with six horses were included for the first time. The rate for sheep and oxen was substantially increased.

Trustees were given power to seize the goods of any traveller refusing to pay the Toll and if the Toll was not paid within two days, the goods could be sold.

There were other sanctions too. Any person seeking to evade the Toll by using another road could be fined twenty shillings! And the Trustees could take to Court any person who should 'Steal, take away, break down or spoil' the turnpikes or tollhouses'. The punishment of those found guilty was severe, including even the possibility of seven years transportation.

The many Turnpike Acts of the 18th century reflected the recognition that roads and their maintenance were vital to the nation's well-being. They also show how, very often, attempted solutions to problems can create their own problems. We in the twentieth century are finding much the same thing!

Chapter 19

DOWN IN THE FOREST
SOMETHING STIRRED

Up in London in 1727 George II was crowned and began his thirty-three year reign. Down in Towcester they celebrated the coronation, but in a somewhat surprising way. They harnessed their horse teams, assembled their ropes and chains and then, armed with axes and saws, they made their way in large numbers into Whittlewood Forest. There, they set to work with a will to fell the mighty oak trees. Before two days had ended they had cut down and carried away no fewer than sixty fine oaks.

The astonishing news had reached them that, to mark the coronation, they could help themselves in the Royal Forest to as much standing timber as they pleased. It was all free, and was theirs for the felling and carting. That was the astonishing news that had reached them.

News? It wasn't news at all – it was mere rumour and it had no foundation whatsoever. How do such rumours start? Who originates them and, as the rumour spreads, who bothers to question it? For the men of Towcester it was a bonanza. And not only in Towcester, but in many other places too, on both sides of the Bucks./Northants. border.

Horrified forest officials did their best to halt this madness, but no one would listen. The timber was free and was theirs for the taking, they told the officials. They said the timber was 'Coronation Poles' and they had been made free of it to mark the King's Coronation, God bless him! There were angry exchanges between the tree-fellers and the forest officials. And the tree felling proceeded apace.

Thomas Herbert was the Woodward, the official in charge of that part of Whittlewood Forest. He was distraught and distracted. With his few forest rangers he rushed madly around begging the tree-fellers to stop. He got only abuse in return – abuse and threats of violence. And the felling went on. Men from fifty or more villages were now at it, and over a hundred oaks had been felled.

Herbert sent frantic messages to London to tell the Surveyor-General what was happening. He asked for urgent help to bring this madness to an end. All he got in reply was an instruction that he was to mark the trees that were felled and to record the villages to which they were taken.

By now Herbert feared for his own safety and for the safety of his few rangers. He sent another urgent plea to London for help, and he added this time that as well as the timber the rioters were now beginning to carry off the deer as well!

In London the Surveyor-General consulted the Attorney-General. And that legal luminary sent word that a selection of rioters should be arrested on a Justice's Warrant and then given exemplary corporal punishment. This, it was hoped, would bring the rest to their senses. The Attorney-General added that if Herbert could not carry out these instructions, he should call out the Redcoats stationed in Towcester.

That did the trick. When the soliders appeared, the tree-fellers desisted. So, after two weeks of rioting, the tree-felling stopped. The bonanza was over. But there was still retribution to come. The prosecutions and court hearings dragged on for months.

The authorities were determined to restore law and order, but they feared to be too harsh lest they make matters worse. So they decided to punish only a selection of the most troublesome and insolent offenders. Others were simply bound over to keep the peace. A sort of amnesty was declared. Any people still in possession of the timber were told they could pay for it, and keep it, and not face charges.

But what about poor Thomas Herbert? The troubles were far from over for him. Daily he was insulted and threatened. All the blame for the prosecutions was laid on his shoulders, and he was warned that he would be killed. He sent frantic messages to his superiors in London begging them to announce publicly that he was in no way to blame for the prosecutions pending for hearing at the Assizes. The delay in hearing the cases made Herbert's plight worse. He dare not leave his house for fear of attack.

At last the cases were heard. The defendants were bound over and were given two weeks in which they must either pay for the timber they had taken, or return it to the forest. The defendants from the Buckinghamshire side of the border complied. Those from Northants. were more obstinate. They announced truculently that they would hang on to the timber they had taken, and would beat up anybody who tried to take it from them.

Some of the timber was stacked in Towcester itself. The law-breakers there were encouraged in their obduracy by the Earl of Pomfret's Steward who refused to let the forest officials take the timber away unless they first paid a fee to the Lord of the Manor for the infringement of his freehold.

Some of the worst offenders simply disappeared, fleeing the countryside. Others did not have the charges for timber stealing pursued against them because they were already in prison for deer-stealing.

Gradually the great 'Coronation Poles' affair died down. Herbert, feeling very hard done by, wrote again to his superior, The Surveyor-General. He felt he was owed compensation for the trauma he had suffered. He asked, not unreasonably, for some monetary award 'for the pains and trouble I had, the hazard I ran in preventing the destruction of the forest'. The Surveyor-General replied that he would consider making Herbert a special allowance. Alas, it was too late. Within six months Herbert was dead. There were dark hints that he had been poisoned and that the rioters had carried out their threats.

But before Herbert died he had handed in the names of those he considered the greatest offenders. And among them was a parson!

The Armed and Dangerous Vicar

The Reverend John Welch, at the height of the timber riots, was told that men from the next parish had felled a mighty oak. They had lopped off all its branches but had not yet carted away the trunk. So the Vicar saw his opportunity. He ordered his servants, and other men from his parish, to go into the forest and to haul the trunk in. That done, the Vicar had the stolen tree trunk concealed in his parish under a hastily constructed haystack.

When the men from the next parish learned how they had been bilked, they went in a body to demand from the Vicar that he should surrender their tree trunk! At the Vicarage they were confronted by the Vicar who made it plain that he had no intention of complying. It did not go unnoticed that when the Vicar said this, he was armed! As well as his gun, the Vicar also had on his side the men of his own parish. The 'owners' of the disputed tree trunk knew they had met their match. They could only mutter and go back to their own village empty-handed.

But that didn't alter the fact that the name of the Reverend John Welch was still on the list of names that Herbert had handed in. No matter. The case never came to court. The sturdy men of John Welch's parish were far too loyal to their Vicar to testify against him. Or perhaps they too, like the men of the next parish, had a healthy respect for the Vicar's gun!

So that is the true story of how, in 1727, 'down in the forest something stirred'.

Chapter 20

MANORS NO MORE

Suitably, this last chapter of 'Manors and Mayhem, Paupers and Parsons' recalls some 'Manors that are no more'. Of the many of which this is true, here are just three, one in Beds., one in Bucks., and one in Northants. The history of all three includes dramatic and often tragic episodes.

Houghton House

In its heyday this lovely house near Ampthill must have been a wonderful sight, with its orange-red bricks and Totternhoe stone. And it was wonderful not only in sight, but also in its site – with the view that it commanded over beautiful countryside looking across to a range of hills.

It was built in 1615 for the Duchess of Pembroke and was altogether splendid. There was a panelled hall, a smoking room and parlour, and a library. Add to these a great dining room, and three other fine chambers which estate agents today would call 'reception rooms' – the withdrawing room, the red damask room and the blue room. There was also a picture gallery and a range of fine bedrooms.

The home farm kept the household in provisions, duck came from a decoy on the estate, and freshwater fish were kept in the park. A kitchen garden and orchard completed the domestic scene. There were gardens too, and a bowling green. Adequate stables housed riding horses and working horses, and there were coach houses. Altogether then, a splendid establishments.

When the Countess of Pembroke died in 1621 the house

Houghton House – ruins of the lovely mansion which inspired John Bunyan.

passed to the Bruce family and was lived in by the Countess of Devonshire. But troublous times lay ahead. In the Civil War of 1642–47 the Countess intrigued for the Royalist cause. When she died her nephew, Robert Bruce, succeeded. He too was an ardent Royalist who shared in the efforts to bring back the exiled Charles to the throne of his executed father. He paid for this support. He was arrested and taken to London, charged with conspiring to bring back Charles. When this was accomplished, in 1660, Charles II made Robert Bruce the Earl of Ailesbury in recognition of his support.

The Earl of Ailesbury became Lord Lieutenant of Bedfordshire in 1664, and soon after that Recorder of Bedford. In 1678 he was made a Privy Councillor. But fate held more troubles in store for Houghton House and its owner.

When Charles II died he was succeeded by his brother, James II. James was an avowed Catholic, intent on restoring the Catholic faith in England. This alarmed many and had prompted the Rye House Plot in 1683 – an attempt to assassinate both Charles II and the future James II. The plot failed. But opposition to James II continued, as the thoughts of

The grand staircase from Houghton House is now in the Swan Hotel in Bedford. (JH)

many turned to his daughter Mary, the wife of William of Orange.

James II abdicated in 1701 and went into exile in France. The Earl of Ailesbury, one of the Gentlemen of the Bedchamber to James, begged the king not to abdicate. When William and Mary were crowned Ailesbury was for a time imprisoned in the Tower, but he was released and returned to Houghton House. But he was relieved of his Lord Lieutenancy and was still much under suspicion for his loyalty to the exiled James. So he too went into exile, and Houghton House, 'that beautiful habitation that I doted on', was shut up.

Moving the story on, in 1738 the Duke of Bedford bought Houghton House, and his son, the Marquess of Tavistock, lived there from 1764 to 1767. The Marques of Tavistock died from a tragic accident in 1767 and the great house again stood empty. In 1794 the Duke of Bedford had the house demolished. The wrought-iron gates of the park are today in Church Street in Ampthill. And the great staircase from Houghton House was installed in The Swan Hotel in Bedford.

So today Houghton House exists only as a ruin. Yet it continues to exist in another way – as a literary reference. John Bunyan, as an itinerant tinker, knew the house well. When he wrote 'Pilgrim's Progress', and described how Pilgrim came to 'The Palace Beautiful' by climbing the 'Hill Difficulty', it was Houghton House that inspired him. And when Bunyan described the sight of 'the delectable mountains' it was the view from Houghton House that prompted his pen. So the lovely house, though a ruin, lives on in Bunyan's immortal work.

Hillesden Manor

The young King Edward VI granted the estate of Hillesden in 1554 to Thomas Denton, an eminent lawyer and Treasurer of the Temple. He made his home there and represented Buckinghamshire in Parliament.

He and his heirs prospered at Hillesden. Within walking

distance lay Claydon House, home of the Verneys. And not far from both were the houses and estates of the Hampdens of Great Hampden, of the Temples of Stowe, and of the Grenvilles of Wootton.

For well over half a century these families – Dentons, Verneys, Hampdens, Temples and Grenvilles – were friends and neighbours. A. L. Rowse, the historian, described their association as 'a close-knit, well-defined cousinage'.

But all that was soon to be shattered as the confrontation between King Charles and his Parliament deepened and finally erupted in Civil War. In that conflict enmity replaced old friendship.

Some, like the Hampdens, led the way in supporting Parliament. Some, like the Verneys, agonised over which side to support. Sir Edmund Verney of Claydon, while his head inclined him to support Parliament, knew in his heart that loyalty required him to support the King, whose Standard Bearer he was. For the Dentons of Hillesden there was no such conflict of conscience. They were out and out Royalists.

The two sides in the Civil War, Cavaliers and Roundheads, marched and manoeuvred, skirmished often, and fought the occasional pitched battle. By 1644 Aylesbury was a great Parliamentarian stronghold, while the Royalists held Oxford which Charles had made his capital.

The Dentons at Hillesden prepared for the worst. They set about fortifying their great house and the Church with it, determined to hold their part of Buckinghamshire for the King. Aware of this, the Roundhead forces at Aylesbury prepared to attack Hillesden. This they did in 1644.

The first assault was on Tuesday, 27th February 1644, and it was inconclusive. So a fresh attack was planned and Cromwell himself was in command. Cromwell led his troops first to Steeple Claydon and camped there on 3rd March 1644. Next day the attack proper was launched. The church was first taken and then the house itself was stormed. Denton's garrison surrendered. The Parliamentary forces gained much by their victory – much ammunition, a great deal of money (found hidden in the wainscotting) and much booty of all kinds.

Then, because it was rumoured that a Royalist force was coming from Oxford to try to recover Hillesden, Cromwell's men set it on fire and reduced it to ruins. Sir Alexander Denton was taken prisoner and died, it is said, of a broken heart. His son, Col. John Denton, was killed in a battle at Abingdon in 1648. But the the Civil War was virtually over, and Cromwell's eleven year rule as Lord Protector followed.

After the Restoration a gradual great sorting out of 'who owns what' took place. In that process Hillesden House rose from its ashes and was rebuilt, though on a much reduced scale. Cole, the Bletchley Diarist, visited the rebuilt Hillesden House and described it as 'a good old house, on a beautiful hill, commanding a delightful prospect'.

But that rebuilt house did not survive. In its turn it was demolished, and today no trace whatever remains of it.

But the church of course is still there, and is indeed one of the finest perpendicular churches in the whole county. In it you can see the bullet holes made by the Roundheads, and see also the many Denton memorials, some of them damaged by Cromwell's soldiers.

There is a slight irony in this survival of the church. In earlier centuries, when the church was under the control of Notely Priory, it was in a fairly ruinous condition. The Priory remonstrated and said that the church must be renovated and made good. This was done to such good effect that the church became what it still is – an architectural gem.

So the house of God, full of Denton memorials, has survived, while Hillesden house itself, the home of the Dentons, is no more.

Fotheringay

Fotheringay in Northamptonshire was more than a Manor, it was a Castle. The execution of Mary Queen of Scots in Fotheringay Castle is one of the most tragic episodes of the 16th century. She was Elizabeth I's cousin. Because Elizabeth had once been declared illegitimate (because her mother was Anne Boleyn), Mary Queen of Scots had once claimed the English crown for herself. So while she still lived, Elizabeth felt insecure.

Troubles of her own in Scotland forced Mary to abdicate the Scottish throne. She fled into England to throw herself on Elizabeth's mercy. While Elizabeth deliberated what to do with her, Mary was kept in Fotheringay Castle as a prisoner.

Reluctantly, Elizabeth decided that Mary must be eliminated. Bull, the London Executioner, was sent up from the capital to carry out the sentence. His orders were that the beheading must not be done in public, so a scaffold was erected in the banqueting hall of the castle. And there, on 8th February 1587 Mary Queen of Scots was put to death.

This tragic event was but the latest of a series of tragedies enacted at Fotheringay. Fotheringay was first built as a Norman stronghold. It was once the home of another Mary, Mary of Valence, whose husband was killed in a tournament on his wedding day.

From Fotheringay Edward Duke of York set out to take part in the French Wars. He was killed at Agincourt. His brother, Richard Duke of Cambridge who succeeded him, was executed. And *his* son, Richard Duke of York, lost his life in the Battle of Wakefield Green. Richard's widow lived on for thirty-six years at Fotheringay, and mourned the deaths of her grandsons, the little Princes murdered in the Tower.

Henry VIII gave the castle to Katherine of Aragon as part of her dowry. When she fell from favour he wanted to keep her at Fotheringay. But Katherine, all too familiar with the many tragedies associated with Fotheringay, refused to live there.

When James I succeeded Elizabeth in 1603 he gave the castle to Lord Newport, who demolished it after James died. So Fotheringay Castle is no more.

Its history has one final strange twist. In 1820 a young contractor was employed to tidy up the ruins. His name was Bob Wyatt. One day, in the stones and rubble, he found a small mud-encrusted object. Astonishingly, it proved to be Mary Queen of Scots' betrothal ring, which evidently had fallen from her hand as she was beheaded. It had lain among the rubble for over two hundred years.

The discovery made Bob Wyatt famous, and for many years he acted as the unofficial guide to the ruins of Fotheringay, the Castle that was no more. He lived to the age of eighty-two, dying in 1861.

INDEX

Books Published by
THE BOOK CASTLE

JOURNEYS INTO BEDFORDSHIRE: Anthony Mackay.
Foreword by The Marquess of Tavistock, Woburn Abbey.
A lavish book of over 150 evocative ink drawings.

A PILGRIMAGE IN HERTFORDSHIRE: H. M. Alderman.
Classic, between-the-wars tour round the county, embellished
with line drawings.

CHILTERN ARCHAEOLOGY: RECENT WORK:
A Handbook for the Next Decade: edited by Robin Holgate.
The latest views, results and excavations by twenty-three
leading archaeologists throughout the Chilterns.

COUNTRYSIDE CYCLING IN BEDFORDSHIRE,
BUCKINGHAMSHIRE and HERTFORDSHIRE: Mick Payne.
Twenty rides on- and off-road for all the family.

LOCAL WALKS: South Bedfordshire and North Chilterns:
Vaughan Basham. Twenty-seven thematic circular walks.

LOCAL WALKS: North and Mid-Bedfordshire:
Vaughan Basham. Twenty-five thematic circular walks.

CHILTERN WALKS: Hertfordshire, Bedfordshire and
North Buckinghamshire: Nick Moon.
CHILTERN WALKS: Buckinghamshire: Nick Moon.
CHILTERN WALKS: Oxfordshire and
West Buckinghamshire: Nick Moon.
A trilogy of circular walks, in association with the Chiltern
Society. Each volume contains thirty circular walks.

OXFORDSHIRE WALKS:
Oxford, the Cotswolds and the Cherwell Valley: Nick Moon.
OXFORDSHIRE WALKS:
Oxford, the Downs and the Thames Valley: Nick Moon.
Two volumes that complement Chiltern Walks: Oxfordshire
and complete coverage of the county, in association with the
Oxford Fieldpaths Society. Thirty circular walks in each.

FOLK: Characters and Events in the History
of Bedfordshire and Northamptonshire: Vivienne Evans.
Anthology about people of yesteryear – arranged alphabetically
by village or town.

LEGACIES:
Tales and Legends of Bedfordshire and Hertfordshire:
Vic Lea. Twenty-five mysteries and stories based on fact,
including Luton Town Football Club. Many photographs.

MANORS and MAYHEM, PAUPERS and POLITICS:
Tales from Four Shires: Beds., Bucks., Herts.,
and Northants.: John Houghton.
Little-known historical snippets and stories.

MYTHS and WITCHES, PEOPLE and POLITICS:
Tales from Four Shires: Bucks., Beds., Herts.,
and Northants.: John Houghton.
Anthology of strange but true historical events.

ECCENTRICS and VILLAINS, HAUNTINGS and HEROES:
Tales from Four Shires: Northants., Beds.,
Bucks., and Herts.: John Houghton.
True incidents and curious events covering one thousand years.

THE RAILWAY AGE IN BEDFORDSHIRE: Fred Cockman.
Classic, illustrated acount of early railway history.

SWANS IN MY KITCHEN: The Story of a Swan Sanctuary:
Lis Dorer. Foreword by Dr Philip Burton. Updated edition.
Tales of her dedication to the survival of these beautiful birds
through her sanctuary near Hemel Hempstead.

WHIPSNADE WILD ANIMAL PARK: 'MY AFRICA': Lucy Pendar.
Foreword by Andrew Forbes. Introduction by Gerald Durrell.
Inside story of sixty years of the Park's animals and people –
full of anecdotes, photographs and drawings.

DUNSTABLE WITH THE PRIORY, 1100–1550: Vivienne Evans.
Dramatic growth of Henry I's important new town around a
major crossroads.

DUNSTABLE DECADE: THE EIGHTIES:
A Collection of Photographs: Pat Lovering.
A souvenir book of nearly 300 pictures of people and events in
the 1980s.

DUNSTABLE IN DETAIL: Nigel Benson.
A hundred of the town's buildings and features, plus town trail
map.

OLD DUNSTABLE: Bill Twaddle.
A new edition of this collection of early photographs.

BOURNE and BRED:
A Dunstable Boyhood Between the Wars: Colin Bourne.
An elegantly written, well-illustrated book capturing the spirit
of the town over fifty years ago.

ROYAL HOUGHTON: Pat Lovering.
Illustrated history of Houghton Regis from the earliest times to
the present.

BEDFORDSHIRE'S YESTERYEARS Vol. 1:
The Family, Childhood and Schooldays:
Brenda Fraser-Newstead.
Unusual early 20th century reminiscences, with private photographs.

BEDFORDSHIRE'S YESTERYEARS Vol. 2:
The Rural Scene: Brenda Fraser-Newstead.
Vivid first-hand accounts of country life two or three generations ago.

BEDFORDSHIRE'S YESTERYEARS Vol. 3:
Craftsmen and Trades People:
Brenda Fraser-Newstead.
Fascinating recollections over several generations practising many vanishing crafts and trades.

BEDFORDSHIRE'S YESTERYEARS Vol. 4:
War Times and Civil Matters:
Brenda Fraser-Newstead.
Two World Wars, plus transport, law and order, etc.

THE CHANGING FACE OF LUTON:
An Illustrated History:
Stephen Bunker, Robin Holgate and Marian Nichols.
Luton's development from earliest times to the present busy industrial town. Illustrated in colour and monochrome. The three authors from Luton Museum are all experts in local history, archaeology, crafts and social history.

THE MEN WHO WORE STRAW HELMETS:
Policing Luton, 1840–1974: Tom Madigan.
Meticulously chronicled history; dozens of rare photographs; author served in Luton Police for nearly fifty years.

BETWEEN THE HILLS:
The Story of Lilley, a Chiltern Village: Roy Pinnock.
A priceless piece of our heritage – the rural beauty remains but the customs and way of life described here have largely disappeared.

GLEANINGS REVISITED:
Nostalgic Thoughts of a Bedfordshire's Farmer's Boy:
E W O'Dell.
His own sketches and early photographs adorn this lively account of rural Bedfordshire in days gone by.

FARM OF MY CHILDHOOD, 1925–1947: Mary Roberts.
An almost vanished lifestyle on a remote farm near Flitwick.

THE VALE OF THE NIGHTINGALE:
The True Story of a Harpenden Family: Molly Andrews.
Victorian times to the present day in this lovely village.

THE TALL HITCHIN SERGEANT:
A Victorian Crime Novel based on fact: Edgar Newman.
Mixes real police officers and authentic background with an exciting storyline.

THE TALL HITCHIN INSPECTOR'S CASEBOOK:
A Victorian Crime Novel based on fact: Edgar Newman.
Worthies of the time encounter more archetypal villains.

LEAFING THROUGH LITERATURE: Writer's Lives
in Hertfordshire and Bedfordshire: David Carroll.
Illustrated short biographies of many famous authors and their connections with these counties.

THE HILL OF THE MARTYR: An Architectural History
of St. Albans Abbey: Eileen Roberts.
Scholarly and readable chronological narrative history of Hertfordshire and Bedfordshire's famous cathedral. Fully illustrated with photographs and plans.

SPECIALLY FOR CHILDREN

VILLA BELOW THE KNOLLS:
A Story of Roman Britain: Michael Dundrow.
An exciting adventure for young John in Totternhoe and Dunstable two thousand years ago.

ADVENTURE ON THE KNOLLS:
A Story of Iron Age Britain: Michael Dundrow.
Excitement on Totternhoe Knolls as ten-year-old John finds himself back in those dangerous times, confronting Julius Caesar and his army.

THE RAVENS:
One Boy Against the Might of Rome: James Dyer.
On the Barton Hills and in the south-east of England as the men of the great fort of Ravensburgh (near Hexton) confront the invaders.

Further titles are in preparation.
All the above are available via any bookshop, or from the publisher and bookseller
THE BOOK CASTLE
12 Church Street, Dunstable Bedfordshire, LU5 4RU
Tel: (01582) 605670